RootGr

"A rose by any other name would smell as sweet"

William Shakespeare
An adage from "Romeo and Juliet"

TABLE OF CONTENTS

Intro 4

Section 1: Low to Medium light plants 6

Aluminum Plant	8	Lucky Bamboo	26
Arrow-Head Plant	9	Nerve Plant	27
Asparagus Fern	10	Parlor Palm	28
Baby Rubber Plant	11	Peace Lily	29
Baby's Tears	12	Prayer Plant	30
Bird's Nest Fern	13	Polka dot plant	32
Boston Fern	14	Rabbit's Foot Fern	33
Chinese Evergreen	15	Rattlesnake Plant	34
Cast Iron Plant	16	Rubber Plant	35
Chinese Money Plant	18	Satin Pothos	36
Christmas Cactus	19	Spider Plant	37
Corn Plant	20	Snake Plant	38
Dieffenbachia	21	Watermelon peperomia	40
English Ivy	22	Wax Plant	41
Golden Pothos	24	Weeping Fig	42
Heartleaf Philodendron	25	ZZ Plant	43

Section 2: Medium light plants 44

African Violet	46	GoldFish Plant	58
Alocasia	47	Heart of jesus	59
Aloe vera	48	Inch Plant	60
Areca Palm	50	Jade Plant	61
Cape Primrose	51	Kalanchoe	62
Common Staghorn Fern	52	Lipstick Plant	63
Croton	53	Lily of the Valley	64
Flame Violet	54	Money Tree	66
Flamingo Flower	55	Moth Orchid	67
Friendship Plant	56	Monstera	68
Gloxinia	57	Norfolk Island Pine	70

Octopus plant	71	Star Jasmine	77
Pink Princess	72	Ti Plant	78
Painted Nettle	73	Umbrella tree	80
Ponytail Palm	74	Urn plant	81
Sago Palm	75	Wax Begonia	82
Scarlet Star	76	Yucca	83

Section 3: Medium to High light plants 84

Air Plant	86	Horseshoe geranium	106
Bird of Paradise	87	Kentia Palm	107
Basil	88	Lemon Balm	108
Calla Lily	90	Living Stones	110
Cape jasmine	91	Madagascar Dragon Tree	111
Common lantana	92	Madagascar Jasmine	112
Cooper's haworthia	93	Majesty Palm	113
Common sage	94	Mexican snow ball	114
Desert Rose	96	Poinsettia	115
Dill	97	Rosemary	116
Evergreen azalea	98	Silver Dollar	118
False shamrock	99	String of pearls	119
Fiddle Leaf Fig	100	Taro	120
Ghost Plant	101	Thyme	122
Garden Marigold	102	Venus Flytrap	124
Hibiscus	104	Zebra Haworthia	125
Hindu Rope	105		

Section 4: The Right Plant for Every Space 126

6 Houseplants for beginners	128	6 fragrant houseplants	140
6 Houseplants for bedroom	130	6 Houseplants for office desk	142
6 Houseplants for bathroom	132	6 Houseplants for dark corners	144
6 Houseplants for Kitchen	134	6 Houseplants to plant in water	146
6 Houseplants for balcony	136	Safe for pets Houseplant	148
6 Houseplants for good luck	138		

The Last Leaf 150

INTRODUCTION

Welcome to the vibrant world of RootGrowings, where every leaf weaves a story, and every plant finds its special place. We are the RootGrowings team, a collective of plant lovers united by our passion for integrating nature's splendor into living spaces. Our journey with houseplants is about more than aesthetics; it's about nurturing relationships with living, green companions that turn any house into a home brimming with life.
In this book, you'll traverse a handpicked selection of 99 houseplants, each detailed with its own story and care guide. These plants are chosen to flourish in environments ranging from the low-light serenity of a quiet corner to the bright embrace of a sunny windowsill. Whether you are a seasoned plant connoisseur or just beginning to let your green thumb emerge, there's a path laid out for you here.

A SANCTUARY OF GREEN
The allure of plants extends beyond their visual charm to their profound capacity to enhance our well-being. They stand as living art, infusing our homes with energy and life. In an era where urban spaces often eclipse nature, RootGrowings stands as a beacon of nature's resilience and its seamless integration into our daily environments.
Venture into the heart of this book, and you'll uncover plants perfectly suited for every unique space in your home, from the steamy comfort of your bathroom to the peaceful ambiance of your bedroom. We'll introduce you to plants that are not only visually stunning but also enrich the air and spirit.

THE HEALTHY HOME
The plants you welcome into your home do wonders—they rejuvenate and inspire. They're the unspoken healers, purifying the air and inviting calmness into our busy lives. Through these pages, you'll learn how the mindful care of your plants can reduce stress and elevate your day, creating a sanctuary for health and happiness.

But our journey is reciprocal—it's about the care we bestow upon our plants as well. This book serves as a thorough guide, imparting the essentials of plant care from lighting to watering, all from a plant-centric viewpoint.

YOUR INDOOR GARDEN

The essence of RootGrowings is connection to nature, to our living spaces, and to the community. It's about cultivating tranquil spots in unexpected places and fostering growth that goes beyond the pot. This book is an invitation to join a community that revels in the beauty of indoor gardening.

We invite every plant enthusiast, from novices to experts, to find inspiration within these pages to create your own verdant retreat. So, let's begin this journey, nurture our seedlings, and watch as our homes transform into lush sanctuaries.

DISCLAIMER:

- The content in this book is based on our personal opinions and experiences.
- For pet safety, please do additional research, as plant toxicity information may change over time.
- Be aware of plant mislabeling: some non-toxic plants may share common names with toxic varieties. Always verify the scientific name for safety.
- You may find slight variations in color, shape, and size of the plants in this book due to natural diversity.
- We list ideal and tolerable lighting conditions. Observe your plants and adjust care to suit their specific needs.

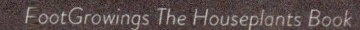

Section 1:
LOW TO MEDIUM LIGHT PLANTS

Thriving in Gentle Illumination: The World of Low to Medium Light Plants

Explore plants suited for low to medium light, perfect for dimly lit areas in homes or offices. These low-maintenance, shade-tolerant plants thrive with minimal sunlight, adding charm to less-illuminated spaces. Learn about their simple care and watering needs. Ideal for shadowed corners or partially sunlit shelves, they bring life and vibrancy to understated spots, transforming them into cozy, inviting areas.

Aluminum Plant
Pilea cadierei (Family: Urticaceae)

 Light	Water	Temparature	Humidity	Pets
Ideal: Full shade Tolerate: Partial sun	Every Week	65-80°F (18-27°C)	High (60-80%)	Safe for Cats and Dogs

CARING GUIDE

Water: Requires consistent, moderate moisture. Water when the top 2 inches start to dry out, without drowning the roots.

Light: Thrives well under sheltered light and can endure limited sunlight. Excessive sunlight may lead to leaf scorching while not enough light might stunt growth.

Fertilization: Use a half-strength balanced liquid fertilizer every 4-6 weeks for the growing season, ending before winter starts.

SUITABLE FOR:
Bedroom, Bathroom, Kitchen, Living Room, Office/Study Room, Children's Room, East or North-facing window

Also known as: Watermelon Pilea, Watermelon Plant

The aluminum plant is the chillest roommate you could ask for! Give it some sunshine and a sip of water now and then, and it'll reward you with its stunning silver-patterned leaves for years to come. This beauty hails from China and Vietnam, but it's happy to call your indoor garden home. Think of it as a low-maintenance friend adding tropical magic to your space.

The Aluminum Plant, scientifically known as Pilea cadierei, was originally found in the tropical rainforests of Vietnam. The Genus (Pilea) is derived from the Latin word "pilus," meaning hair, possibly referring to the tiny hairs on the leaves and stems of many Pilea species. The species (cadierei) is named after R.P. Cadière, a Belgian missionary who discovered the plant in Vietnam. It was later introduced to the Western world. The common name (Aluminum Plant) comes from the silvery patches on its green leaves, which resemble aluminum. The Aluminum Plant, like many Pilea species, is often associated with friendship. This is due to the ease with which it can be propagated and shared among friends.

ARROW-HEAD PLANT

Syngonium podophyllum (Family: Araceae)

 **LIGHT**
Ideal: Full Shade
Tolerate: Partial sun

 WATER
Every Week

 TEMPERATURE
65-75°F (18-24°C)

HUMIDITY
Moderate (40-60%)

 **PETS**
Not Safe for Cats and Dogs

Also known as: American evergreen, Nephthytis

Enhance your home with the captivating Arrowhead plant, a gem from the Araceae family. This remarkable foliage plant, revered for its air-purifying and striking beauty, has become a beloved choice for houseplant enthusiasts. While its delicate nature necessitates caution around little ones and furry friends, the Arrowhead plant remains a charming, versatile addition to any indoor space.

The Arrowhead Plant (Syngonium podophyllum) is native to a wide region of Latin America from Mexico through Bolivia. The name "Syngonium podophyllum" is derived from the Greek words "syn" (together) and "gone" (womb), hinting at the plant's unique leaf structure where the juvenile leaves are distinctively lobed like an arrowhead. Podophyllum, from "foot" and "leaf," reflects the shape of its petioles. The first scientific description of the plant is attributed to Austrian botanist Heinrich Wilhelm Schott in 1829. This botanical marvel has also earned the moniker "Nephthytis," drawing inspiration from the Egyptian goddess Nephthys, known for her protective and nurturing qualities.

CARING GUIDE

Water: Water regularly, and the soil should dry out in between watering, as this plant is susceptible to overwatering.

Light: Flourishes in areas with limited light. Can tolerate moderate amount of sun, but excessive sunshine exposure could result in yellowing or curling of leaves.

Fertilization: Should be fertilized with a balanced, water-soluble fertilizer during the growing season between spring and fall.

SUITABLE FOR:

Bedroom, Bathroom, Kitchen, Living Room, Office/Study Room, East or North-facing window

Asparagus Fern

Asparagus aethiopicus (Family: Asparagaceae)

 Light	Water	Temperature	Humidity	 Pets
Ideal: Partial sun Tolerate: Full sun, Full shade	Every Week	60-70°F (15-21°C)	High (60-80%)	Not Safe for Cats and Dogs

CARING GUIDE

Water: Needs watering frequently. Water when the topsoil is dry, allow it to drain. Water once a week in most climates.

Light: Thrives best in areas where the sun isn't overly strong, Tolerating complete shade and also sun exposure. Its origin in diverse light environments explains that.

Fertilization: A water-soluble or liquid plant food (5-10-10) that has been diluted by 50% will be required to be given monthly.

SUITABLE FOR:
Bedroom, Bathroom, Kitchen, Living Room, Office/Study Room, Balcony/Patio, East or North-facing window

Also known as: Sprenger's asparagus fern, African asparagus

Hailing from the sun-kissed shores of South Africa, the Sprenger's Asparagus Fern, despite its name, is not a true fern but rather a charming member of the asparagus family. Often mistaken for its fern cousins, this beauty has gained notoriety as an ornamental plant. However, its captivating charm comes with a caveat: it's considered an invasive species in many regions.

Asparagus aethiopicus, also known as Sprenger's asparagus, is a branching perennial herb native to the Cape Provinces and Northern South Africa. Asparagus fern, asparagus grass, and foxtail fern are common names for this plant, but it is unrelated to true ferns. The species was initially described by Carl Linnaeus in 1767, and the attribution "Sprenger's Asparagus" refers to Carl Ludwig Sprenger, who made it popular in Europe as an ornamental plant. In ancient folklore, the Asparagus fern is often associated with various tales of protection and good fortune, believed by some to ward off evil spirits, and carrying a sprig of the plant can bring luck and prosperity.

BABY RUBBER PLANT
Peperomia obtusifolia (Family: Piperaceae)

 **Light**
Ideal: Full Shade
Tolerate: Partial sun

 Water
Every
Week

 Temperature
60-75°F
(15-24°C)

 Humidity
Moderate
(40-50%)

 Pets
Safe for Cats
and Dogs

Also known as: Pepper Face, American Rubber Plant

The beautiful Baby Rubber Plant looks a lot like a miniature version of the Rubber Plant. It's a bushy plant that stands upright with thick stems and shiny, rounded leaves. It grows well in low light or under office lights, which makes it great for places that don't get much sunlight. This charming plant also gets small, off-white flowers on stems that are a reddish-brown color

The Baby Rubber Plant, known scientifically as Peperomia obtusifolia, s native to the tropical rainforests of South America. The genus "Peperomia" is derived from the Greek words "peperi" (pepper) and "homoios" (resembling), indicating its resemblance to the pepper plant. The species "obtusifolia" is Latin for "blunt-leaved," This likely refers to the rounded, non-pointed shape of the leaves. The common name "Baby Rubber Plant" likely comes from its thick, rubbery leaves, though unrelated to the rubber tree used in commercial rubber production. In some cultures, keeping a Peperomia plant, including the Baby Rubber Plant, is believed to bring good luck, especially when given as a gift.

> **CARING GUIDE**
>
> **Water:** Water regularly between spring and fall. Plants that are kept in well-lit areas should be watered more frequently.
>
> **Light:** Thrives with limited sunlight, Found in habitats with filtered light, it can struggle in full sun or complete darkness. Balanced light is key in its life cycle.
>
> **Fertilization:** Use a balanced Fertilizer and if also contains calcium. Feed it once or twice during the summer growing season.

> **SUITABLE FOR:**
> Bedroom, Bathroom, Kitchen, Living Room, Office/Study Room, Children's Room, East or North-facing window

Baby's Tears
Soleirolia soleirolii (Family: Urticaceae)

Light	Water	🌡 Temparature	Humidity	Pets
Ideal: Partial sun Tolerate: Full shade	Every Week	60-70°F (15-21°C)	Moderate (50-60%)	Safe for Cats and Dogs

Also known as: Mind-Your-Own-Business, Angel's Tears

This little charmer called Baby's Tears is a survival champion! It constantly throws out mini versions of itself along its leaf edges; these tiny plantlets even sprout roots while still snuggling up to the mama plant. Who needs flowers when you're this good at making friends? If Baby's Tears feels like showing off, it might surprise you with a sprinkle of pink or grey blooms.

Baby's Tears (Soleirolia soleirolii) is native to the Mediterranean region. The genus name, as well as the species name "Soleiroloa," are derived from Joseph Francois Soleirol, a French botanist known for his botanical exploration. The name "Baby's Tears" likely originates from the small, round leaves of the plant, which resemble tiny teardrops. This name evokes the delicate nature of the plant. It is also known as Mind-Your-Own-Business, humorously suggests the plant's vigorous and creeping nature as it spreads and fills spaces with green lushness, politely minding its own business. In some cultures, the plant is associated with the idea of nurturing and growth, capturing the essence of tender care for a garden.

CARING GUIDE

Water: Keep the soil always moist. Water well throughout the summer, and ensure the roots do not dry out in the winter.

Light: Prefers moderate sun exposure but can also exist comfortably in more shady areas. Too much sun can result in damage, while too little might hinder its growth.

Fertilization: Fertilize every month during the spring and summer. Use a liquid balanced plant fertilizer to get the best results.

SUITABLE FOR:
Bedroom, Bathroom, Kitchen, Living Room, Office/Study Room, Children's Room, East or North-facing window

BIRD'S NEST FERN
Asplenium Nidus (Family: Aspleniaceae)

 **LIGHT**
Ideal: full shade
Tolerate: Partial sun

 WATER
Every
Week

 TEMPERATURE
65-80°F
(18-27°C)

 **HUMIDITY**
High
(60-70%)

 PETS
Safe for Cats
and Dogs

Also known as: Nest fern, Rumah Langsuyar

The bird's-nest fern, or Asplenium nidus for science lovers, might hail from tropical Asia, but it's a homebody at heart. Its secret weapon? That lush, central rosette where its fronds unfurl like a cozy nest cradling tiny green eggs. This beautiful marvel just needs a splash of water now and then, and it'll reward you with lush, prehistoric vibes all year round.

The Bird's Nest Fern (Asplenium nidus) is native to tropical regions of Asia, East Africa, and Australia. The genus name "Asplenium" derives from the Greek word "a-," meaning "without," and "splen" meaning "spleen." It was historically believed that these plants were beneficial in treating diseases of the spleen. The species name "nidus" is Latin for "nest," referring to the plant's nest-like rosette of leaves. The Bird's Nest Fern has primarily been appreciated for its ornamental value. However, in some cultures, parts of the plant have been used in traditional medicine. For instance, in some Asian cultures, it's believed to have medicinal properties and has been used to treat ailments like asthma and bruises.

CARING GUIDE

Water: The center of the plant should not be covered in water, to avoid mold, try to water just the surrounding soil.

Light: Thrives in locations minimally exposed to light. It can also tolerate some sun exposure. Despite this, intense light can negatively affect the plant's health.

Fertilization: Fertilize it only during the late spring to early fall growing season. Use a balanced diluted liquid fertilizer.

SUITABLE FOR:
Bedroom, Bathroom, Kitchen, Living Room, Office/Study Room, Children's Room, East or North-facing window

BOSTON FERN
Nephrolepis exaltata (FAMILY: Nephrolepidaceae)

☀ LIGHT	 WATER	🌡 TEMPARATURE	% HUMIDITY	🐾 PETS
Ideal: Partial sun Tolerate: Full sun, Full shade	Twice per week	65-75°F (18-24°C)	Moderate (50-60%)	Safe for Cats and Dogs

CARING GUIDE

Water: Water consistently at the soil level, avoiding the fronds. Water after the first inch of topsoil has become dry.

Light: Prefers moderate sunlight, and can tolerate minimal or generous sunlight. Excessive sun causes leaf discoloration, while too little might affect its development

Fertilization: Fertilize monthly between spring and early fall, with a balanced fertilizer diluted to half its normal strength.

SUITABLE FOR:
Bedroom, Bathroom, Kitchen, Living Room, Office/Study Room, Children's Room, East or North-facing window

Also known as: Sword Fern, Wild Boston Fern

Introducing the Boston Fern, your chill jungle cutie from the tropics! This leafy legend, you might know as "Sword Fern," is a total houseplant superstar. It's down-to-earth, surviving even when things get dry, but it really digs the humidity, so give it a little mist now and then. It's also a total sweetheart - no toxins here, just pure pet-friendly charm.

One theory suggests that the fern gained its name during the Victorian era. It is thought that a Boston-based nursery or florist may have played a significant role in popularizing this particular fern variety, leading to it being referred to as the Boston Fern. Another theory is that "Boston" was used during this period to denote something stylish or fashionable. Therefore, the Boston Fern might have been named as such to convey its popularity and elegance. The genus name Nephrolepis is derived from the Greek words "nephros," meaning kidney, and "lepis," meaning scale. This refers to the kidney-shaped protective structures covering the spore-bearing structures found on the undersides of the fern fronds.

CHINESE EVERGREEN
Aglaonema commutatum (FAMILY: Araceae)

 **LIGHT**
Ideal: Full Shade
Tolerate: Partial sun

 WATER
Every
Week

 TEMPARATURE
60-80°F
(15-27°C)

 **HUMIDITY**
High
(60-80%)

 PETS
Not Safe for
Cats and Dogs

Also known as Poison dart plant

Often mistaken for its close cousin, the dumb cane, the Chinese evergreen is a true beauty in its own right. This hardy houseplant boasts elegant, narrow dark green leaves adorned with subtle light green stripes, a distinguishing feature from its broader-leaved counterpart. Its evergreen nature ensures a year-round splash of greenery, adding a touch of calmness to any indoor or outdoor space.

Chinese Evergreen, known scientifically as Aglaonema commutatum, is native to Asia's tropical and subtropical regions. The genus name "Aglaonema" is derived from two Greek words: "aglaos," meaning bright or shining, and "nema," meaning a thread or filament, possibly referring to the striking stamens of the flowers. "commutatum" is Latin, meaning "changed" which may refer to variations in its leaf patterns. One of the most notable aspects of the Chinese Evergreen is its ability to purify air. It was included in NASA's Clean Air Study, which identified it as effective in removing common toxins like benzene and formaldehyde from the air. This feature makes it an excellent plant for improving indoor air quality.

CARING GUIDE

Water: Let the soil dry out completely between waterings. Water it once a week during spring and summer, less otherwise.

Light: Has its roots in environments with limited sunlight, making it thrive in lower light conditions. Providing a small amount of sunlight can be beneficial.

Fertilization: Fertilize once a month or six weeks with a balanced, liquid fertilizer diluted by half in spring and summer only.

SUITABLE FOR:
Bedroom, Bathroom, Kitchen, Living Room, Office/Study Room, East or North-facing window

Cast Iron Plant

Aspidistra elatior (FAMILY: Asparagaceae)

 **Light**
Ideal: full shade
Tolerate: partial sun

 Water
Every
Week

 **Temperature**
50-70°F
(10-21°C)

 Humidity
Moderate
(40-50%)

 Pets
Safe for Cats
and Dogs

Also known as: Bar Room Plant, Ballroom Plant, Iron Plant

Meet the cast-iron plant, the ultimate chill roommate. This Japanese native is a total trooper, surviving on sunshine and neglect like a champ. Don't let the "cast-iron" name fool you; it's actually a flowering beauty with deep green, glossy leaves. Just be warned, its laid-back attitude might attract some unwanted attention from fungus gnats. But hey, even supermodels have flaws, right?

The Cast Iron Plant's ability to thrive in low-light conditions and withstand neglect may symbolize resilience, endurance, and adaptability. The name "Cast Iron Plant" is derived from its reputation for being an exceptionally hardy and durable plant. This common name underscores the plant's ability to thrive in challenging conditions akin to the durability of cast iron materials. The genus name "Aspidistra" is of Greek origin, with "aspidion" meaning "shield"

CARING GUIDE

Water: Prefers medium soil moisture. However, it is a flexible plant that can withstand irregular watering and drought.

Light: The cast iron plant flourishes in shaded areas, away from direct sunlight, maintaining its health in dimly lit spots. It originates from dense, forested habitats.

Fertilization: Does not need regular fertilization. Treat with an all-purpose liquid or slow-release fertilizer in growing season.

SUITABLE FOR:
Bedroom, Bathroom, Kitchen, Living Room, Office/Study Room, Children's Room, East or North-facing window

or "round shield." This name likely refers to the plant's large, sturdy leaves, which are somewhat reminiscent of a shield. The Cast Iron Plant became a popular indoor plant during the Victorian era when it was commonly used as a decorative houseplant. Its ability to thrive in the low-light conditions of Victorian homes made it a practical choice. Nowadays, due to its minimalist aesthetic and ease of care, the Cast Iron Plant has become a favorite among interior designers, especially for industrial and contemporary styles. The plant is mentioned in the novel "The Cast-Iron Shore" by Linda Grant, where the protagonist's mother tends to a Cast Iron Plant. In the novel, the Cast Iron Plant serves as a symbolic element, possibly representing resilience, endurance, or tenacity. The plant's reference might be metaphorical, drawing parallels between the plant's ability to thrive in challenging conditions and the characters' struggles in the narrative.

CHINESE MONEY PLANT
Pilea peperomioides (FAMILY: Urticaceae)

LIGHT	WATER	TEMPARATURE	HUMIDITY	 PETS
Ideal: Partial sun Tolerate: Full shade	Every Week	60-80°F (15-27°C)	Moderate (40-60%)	Safe for Cats and Dogs

CARING GUIDE

Water: Let the soil dry out a little between waterings, especially during the cooler months. Keep soil very lightly moist.

Light: Growth benefits from morning's gentler rays while safely avoiding the afternoon's stronger illumination. it can nonetheless flourish in more shaded conditions.

Fertilization: Fertilize once a month during spring, and summer using an all-purpose 20-20-20 fertilizer diluted to half strength.

SUITABLE FOR:
Bedroom, Kitchen, Living Room, Office/Study Room, Children's Room, East or North-facing window

Also known as: Pancake plant, coin plant, or UFO plant

The Chinese money plant boasts big circular leaves, making it a visually appealing indoor plant. With leaves larger than 15 cm across, they are the main attraction. The plant does yield a little white bloom, but its distinct coin-like leaves steal the show. Many Feng Shui followers favor the Chinese money plant, believing it brings good vibes and enhances homes with positive energy.

The Chinese Money Plant, scientifically known as Pilea peperomioides, boasts a rich tapestry of folklore. Hailing from southwestern China's Yunnan province, this green gem has earned various monikers, including the UFO Plant for its saucer-like leaves and Pancake Plant thanks to its flat, round foliage. Its most famous name stems from its supposed association with wealth and prosperity. Legend has it that a Norwegian missionary, Agnar Espegren, brought the plant back from China in the 1940s and began sharing its offshoots as a token of good luck. Despite its popularity as a houseplant, Pilea peperomioides is surprisingly rare in its natural habitat and is considered endangered in the wild in China.

CHRISTMAS CACTUS

Schlumbergera bridgesii (FAMILY: Cactaceae)

LIGHT	WATER	TEMPARATURE	HUMIDITY	PETS
Ideal: Partial sun Tolerate: Full shade	Every 2 weeks	60-70°F (15-21°C)	Moderate (50-60%)	Safe for Cats and Dogs

Also known as: Crab Cactus, Holiday Cactus

Meet the Christmas cactus. This festive cutie hails from the mountains of southeastern Brazil, but it's traded in its wild ways for a life of indoor cheer. Unlike its desert cousins, this cactus thrives with a touch of moisture, so keep that top inch of soil happy! It's been brightening European homes since the 1800s, but watch out - aphids and mealybugs might also want to join the party.

As the name suggests, the Christmas Cactus is often associated with the holiday season, particularly Christmas. Its ability to bloom in winter and produce colorful flowers during the festive period makes it a popular choice for holiday decorations. The genus name "Schlumbergera" was named in honor of Frédéric Schlumberger, a French collector of cacti and succulents in the 19th century. Schlumberger was particularly interested in the cacti of Brazil. The species name "bridgesii" is an epithet that pays tribute to Thomas Bridges, an English missionary who lived in South America in the 19th century. Bridges was an avid naturalist known for his contributions to the study of the flora and fauna of South America.

CARING GUIDE

Water: Water when the top 3 cm of soil dry out, allowing the soil to dry out at least half way down between waterings.

Light: Prefers muted light rather than extreme sunlight exposures, fostering the healthiest growth. In its original habitat, it adapts well to low-light surroundings.

Fertilization: Fertilize monthly with an all-purpose or houseplant fertilizer every 2-4 weeks from early spring to mid-summer.

SUITABLE FOR:

Bedroom, Bathroom, Kitchen, Living Room, Office/Study Room, Balcony/Patio, East or North-facing window

Corn Plant

Dracaena fragrans (Family: Asparagaceae)

☀ LIGHT	💧 WATER	🌡 TEMPERATURE	% HUMIDITY	🐾 PETS
Ideal: Partial sun Tolerate: Full sun, Full shade	Every 2 weeks	60-80°F (15-27°C)	Low (20-40%)	Not Safe for Cats and Dogs

CARING GUIDE

Water: The corn plant should be allowed to dry partially between waterings, but its soil must never become completely dry.

Light: Demands a balance of light, tolerating ample shine to shadowy nooks. Extreme rays scorches the foliage, Lack of sufficient light result in less vibrant foliage.

Fertilization: A balanced liquid fertilizer is ideal for feeding this species, in the growing season between spring and summer.

SUITABLE FOR:
Bedroom, Bathroom, Kitchen, Living Room, Office/Study Room, East or North-facing window

Also known as: Cornstalk Plant, Striped Dracaena

With its glossy green foliage that resembles corn leaves, the Corn Plant is a classic houseplant that adds a touch of tropical classiness to any space. This exotic evergreen beauty, slow-growing perennial shrub is native to tropical Africa but has been a popular houseplant in Europe since the 1800s. Its thick cane, topped by a rosette of lush leaves, gives it the nickname "False Palm Tree."

The Corn Plant, scientifically known as Dracaena fragrans, is a popular houseplant known for its ease of care and attractive appearance. The genus name "Dracaena" is derived from the Greek word "drakaina," which means "female dragon." This is likely a reference to the red gum-like resin in the stems of some species, which was likened to a dragon's blood. The species name "fragrans" translates to 'fragrant' in Latin, referring to the sweet-smelling flowers the plant occasionally produces. While it's known for its foliage, the Corn Plant can produce flowers, although it's rare in indoor environments. When it does bloom, the flowers are highly fragrant, especially at night, releasing a strong and sweet scent.

DIEFFENBACHIA
Dieffenbachia seguine (Family: Araceae)

 **LIGHT**	**WATER**	**TEMPARATURE**	**HUMIDITY**	 **PETS**
Ideal: Full Shade Tolerate: Partial sun	Every 1-2 weeks	60-75°F (15-24°C)	Moderate (40-60%)	Not Safe for Cats and Dogs

Also known as: Dumb Cane, Tuftroot

Dieffenbachia is a true tropical charmer with its captivating beauty and stunning foliage, often adorned with vibrant variegations. While this plant produces showy white blooms, it only flowers under ideal conditions. Please exercise caution when handling Dieffenbachia, as its sap is poisonous and can cause temporary speechlessness for up to two weeks by affecting the throat and vocal cords.

Dieffenbachia seguine, commonly known as Dumbcane or Tuftroot, is a species of Dieffenbachia native to the tropical Americas, ranging from southern Mexico to northern South America. It is also native to Caribbean islands, including Puerto Rico. The genus Dieffenbachia was named after Herr Joseph Dieffenbach. It is believed that Dieffenbach brought Dieffenbachia seguine to Austria from Brazil around 1830 as part of the Austro-Brazilian expeditions (1817-35). Dieffenbachia seguine contains calcium oxalate crystals, which may cause irritation and swelling when chewed or ingested. This has led to one of its common names, "Dumbcane," referring to the temporary speechlessness that can occur after chewing the plant's leaves.

CARING GUIDE

Water: Water when the top two inches of soil are dry. The soil should be kept lightly moist throughout the growing season.

Light: Thrives in low-light, similar to its habitat under dense forest canopies. Insufficient light can hinder its growth, while excessive light can scorch its leaves.

Fertilization: Use a 20-20-20 balanced fertilizer. It should be applied every four to six weeks during the active growing season.

SUITABLE FOR:
Bedroom, Bathroom, Kitchen, East or North-facing window

ENGLISH IVY
Hedera helix (FAMILY: Araliaceae)

LIGHT	WATER	TEMPERATURE	HUMIDITY	PETS
Ideal: Partial sun Tolerate: Full sun, Full shade	Every Week	50–75°F (10–24°C)	Moderate (40–60%)	Not Safe for Cats and Dogs

Also known as: Common Ivy, European Ivy, True Ivy

English ivy is a vigorously perennial woody vine with dark, shiny leaves that retain color throughout the year. This tenacious climber skillfully employs aerial rootlets to grasp tree bark firmly, enabling it to ascend to impressive heights of over 15 meters. Beyond its role as a forest groundcover, English ivy has also established itself as an invasive species outside its native range.

English Ivy, known scientifically as Hedera helix, is a plant rich in history, folklore, and practical uses. The name "Hedera" is derived from the Latin word for ivy, while "helix" is from the Greek word for "twist" or "turn," referring to its climbing habit. In Greek and Roman mythology, English Ivy held a place of honor as a symbol closely associated with Dionysus/Bacchus, the god of wine, ecstasy, and the liberating power of nature. The god was often depicted

CARING GUIDE

Water: Make sure not to overwater, cause it is susceptible to root rot. Water when the first half inch of topsoil is dry.

Light: Wide light tolerance, from ample sun to low light. Thriving in partially sunny conditions that mimic its forest origins, enduring both full sunlight and shade.

Fertilization: Fertilization should be limited to once or twice during the growing season. Use Nitrogen-containing fertilizers.

SUITABLE FOR:
Bedroom, Bathroom, Kitchen, Living Room, Office/Study Room, Balcony/Patio, East or North-facing window.

wearing a crown of ivy and carrying a staff entwined with ivy and topped with a pinecone. In Celtic stories, ivy was seen as a symbol of determination and strength due to its ability to grow in challenging conditions. In some Celtic stories and traditions, ivy is closely associated with holly. Holly and ivy together represent the duality and balance of masculine (holly) and feminine (ivy) energies in nature, a concept important in Celtic belief systems. In the past, it was believed that growing ivy on buildings would protect the structure from misfortune and lightning strikes. Ivy has been mentioned in various literary works across centuries. William Shakespeare often used ivy as a symbol in his plays. For example, in "A Midsummer Night's Dream," ivy represents wedded love and friendship. Historically, ivy was used for a range of medicinal purposes, including as an anti-inflammatory agent and for respiratory conditions like bronchitis.

Golden Pothos
Epipremnum aureum (Family: Araceae)

 Light	Water	Temperature	Humidity	Pets
Ideal: Full Shade Tolerate: Partial sun	Every 1-2 weeks	65-80°F (18-27°C)	Moderate (40-60%)	Not Safe for Cats and Dogs

Also known as: Taro vine, Ivy arum, Hunter's robe

A true survivor, the Golden Pothos is a popular houseplant that thrives in homes worldwide. This beauty was nicknamed "Devil's Ivy" for its resilience; it even tolerates challenging low-light conditions. Its heart-shaped leaves, adorned with splashes of gold, make it a stunning addition to any décor. However, keep it out of reach of pets and children due to its poisonous sap.

The Golden Pothos is scientifically known as "Epipremnum aureum ." The genus Name "Epipremnum" is derived from Greek, where "epi" means upon and "premnon" means a trunk, referring to its growth habit, often climbing on other trees or structures. The species name "aureum" is Latin for golden, a reference to the variegation of its leaves. The term "Pothos" is often used for several plants in the Araceae family. It's thought to be derived from a Greek word which generally refers to longing or yearning. The name "Pothos" is used in horticulture for plants with vining and climbing habits. It's commonly known as devil's ivy due to its remarkable ability to thrive in almost any environment and remain green even in darkness.

Caring Guide

Water: Water every 1-2 weeks. When the soil feel dry one to two inches below the surface, it is time to water your plant.

Light: Thrives in areas with dim lighting and adapts well to partially shaded environments. Evolution with limited sunlight environment has reinforced this inclination.

Fertilization: Fertilize once a month during the spring and summer using a 10-10-10 fertilizer. Do not fertilize during winter.

Suitable for:
Bedroom, Bathroom, Kitchen, Living Room, Office/Study Room, East or North-facing window

Heartleaf Philodendron

Philodendron hederaceum (Family: Araceae)

☀ LIGHT	💧 WATER	🌡 TEMPARATURE	% HUMIDITY	🐾 PETS
Ideal: Full Shade Tolerate: Partial sun	Every Week	60-80°F (15-27°C)	Moderate (40-60%)	Not Safe for Cats and Dogs

Also known as: Sweetheart Plant, Cordatum, Heartleaf

Hailing from the West Indies, the philodendron hederaceum is an evergreen climbing plant that has seamlessly found its way into many homes as a beloved houseplant. Known for its glossy, heart-shaped leaves, this beloved plant adds a tropical elegance to any indoor space. However, it's important to note that it contains calcium oxalate crystals, making it mildly toxic if ingested.

The Heartleaf Philodendron native to Central America and the Caribbean, known scientifically as Philodendron hederaceum, has a rich history and symbolism. The name "Philodendron" comes from the Greek words "Phileo," which means "love," and "dendron," which translates to "tree." This is fitting since P. hederaceum tends to grow upwards, often climbing trees. In ancient Greece, philodendrons symbolized wisdom and knowledge. They are seen as symbols of love and affection in more modern contexts. There's a belief that the Heartleaf Philodendron attracts joy and positivity to any living space it occupies. Giving or receiving this plant as a gift is thought to convey deep emotions.

> **CARING GUIDE**
>
> **Water:** Water regularly in a well-draining pot. The soil around the roots should be allowed to dry out between watering.
>
> **Light:** Prefers areas shielded from intense sunlight, but can sustain moderate sunlight. Originally thriving in shaded areas, it is adapted to lower sunlight intensity.
>
> **Fertilization:** Fertilize regularly during the growing season, in spring and fall. A balanced, houseplant fertilizer, is ideal.

> **SUITABLE FOR:**
> Bedroom, Bathroom, Kitchen, Living Room, Office/Study Room, East or North-facing window

Lucky Bamboo

Dracaena sanderiana (Family: Asparagaceae)

LIGHT	WATER	TEMPARATURE	HUMIDITY	 PETS
Ideal: Partial sun Tolerate: Full shade	Every Week	60-75°F (15-24°C)	Moderate (50-60%)	Not Safe for Cats and Dogs

CARING GUIDE

Water: If grown in water, its roots should be submerged. If grown in soil, keep the always soil moist. Use purified water.

Light: Prefers moderate sunlight, and tolerates full shade. Excessively intense light may stress this plant, whereas insufficient light could slow down its growth.

Fertilization: Apply diluted all-purpose fertilizer sparingly (a few times a year) to prevent overfertilization and root damage.

SUITABLE FOR:
Bedroom, Bathroom, Kitchen, Living Room, Office/Study Room, Children's Room, East or North-facing window

Also known as: Belgian evergreen, Sander's Dracaena

The Lucky Bamboo, an emblem of good luck and prosperity, is a popular plant in many homes. Its elegant, bamboo-like appearance makes it a favorite for adding a touch of greenery and positive energy. It thrives in simple water vases and requires minimal care, making it perfect for busy plant owners. In Feng Shui, positioning the Lucky Bamboo correctly can enhance its beneficial properties.

Lucky Bamboo, scientifically known as Dracaena sanderiana, is a fascinating plant. Despite its name, Lucky Bamboo is not a bamboo at all but rather a member of the Dracaena family. Originating from Africa, particularly in the rainforests of Cameroon, Lucky Bamboo has gained global popularity as an ornamental plant believed to bring good luck. Its name is derived from the resemblance of its stalks to true Bamboo, but the "lucky" association is deeply embedded in Chinese culture, where the number of stalks in an arrangement carries specific symbolic meanings. According to Chinese folklore, the number three is considered especially auspicious, representing happiness, wealth, and longevity.

NERVE PLANT
Fittonia albivenis (FAMILY: Acanthaceae)

 LIGHT	 WATER	TEMPERATURE	HUMIDITY	PETS
Ideal: Partial sun Tolerate: full shade	Every Week	65-75°F (18-24°C)	High (60-70%)	Safe for Cats and Dogs

Also known as: Silver-nerve plant, Silver-threads

Nerve Plant leaves are like miniature masterpieces, with veins like tiny works of art. They flourish best when kept cozy and hydrated with regular watering. Give it the attention it craves, and it'll reward you with stunning foliage. So, if you're searching for a unique houseplant that combines beauty with a touch of the exotic, the nerve plant might just be your ideal choice.

The Nerve Plant (Fittonia albivenis) boasts strikingly patterned leaves that resemble delicate veins, earning it the name "Nerve Plant." Originating from the rainforests of South America, its genus name, Fittonia, pays homage to the 19th-century botanist Elizabeth Fitton. The Nerve Plant (Fittonia albivenis) derives its name from the distinctive patterns of veins that resemble a network of nerves on its leaves. The term "nerve" in its common name refers to these prominent, intricate veins that run across the surface of the leaves. The specific epithet "albivenis" in the scientific name Fittonia albivenis also provides a clue to its name. In Latin, "albi" means white, and "venis" or "venus" means vein.

CARING GUIDE

Water: Water moderately, allowing the soil to dry out in between. Overwatering can cause root rot and leaf spot disease.

Light: Prefers medium-light exposure, which is essential for nurturing its vibrant foliage. It can also tolerate shady conditions. Too much light can cause leaf burn.

Fertilization: Fertilizing monthly with a balanced 5-5-5 fertilizer diluted to half strength in growing season will be sufficient.

SUITABLE FOR:
Bedroom, Bathroom, Kitchen, Living Room, Office/Study Room, Children's Room, East or North-facing window

Parlor Palm
Chamaedorea elegans (Family: Arecaceae)

 Light	Water	Temperature	Humidity	 Pets
Ideal: Partial sun Tolerate: Full shade	Every 1-2 weeks	60-75°F (15-24°C)	Moderate (50-60%)	Safe for Cats and Dogs

CARING GUIDE

Water: Water when the first two inches of soil dry out, or once a week, and shift to twice-monthly if it is cool enough.

Light: Prefers filtered sun, relishing the rays that doesn't hit it harshly. It tolerates lesser sunlit environments, but lack of light might lead to stunted growth.

Fertilization: Fertilize parlor palm with a water-soluble houseplant fertilizer every 3-4 weeks during the active growing season.

SUITABLE FOR:
Bedroom, Bathroom, Kitchen, Living Room, Office/Study Room, Balcony/Patio, East or North-facing window

Also known as: Neanthe Bella Palm, Collinia elegans

With its vibrant tropical fronds, the Parlor palm is perfect for beginners. It flourishes best in tropical or indoor environments with bright, indirect light but adapts well to lower light. This palm effectively purifies the air, adds humidity, and brings an attractive touch of green to your space. It can live indoors and even longer outdoors for several decades in appropriate climates.

The Parlor Palm (Chamaedorea elegans), also known as the Neanthe Bella Palm, is native to the rainforests of Southern Mexico and Guatemala. It was popularized during the Victorian era as a symbol of sophistication and luxury, earning its moniker "Parlor Palm" for its favored place in Victorian parlors. The genus name "Chamaedorea" is derived from the Greek words "chamai" (on the ground) and "dorea" (gift), implying a gift on the ground or a humble gift. This reflects the plant's small stature compared to other palms. Its specific epithet, "elegans," aptly captures its graceful appearance. The Parlor Palm's versatility extends to its other names, like "Neanthe Bella," conveying a sense of beauty and charm.

PEACE LILY
Spathiphyllum wallisii (FAMILY: Araceae)

 LIGHT	WATER	TEMPERATURE	 HUMIDITY	PETS
Ideal: Full Shade Tolerate: Partial sun	Every Week	65-80°F (18-27°C)	High (60-80%)	Not Safe for Cats and Dogs

Also known as: White Sails, Closet Plant, Spathe Flower

The Peace Lily is an elegant plant known for its lush green leaves and white, spoon-shaped flowers. It's a low-maintenance plant that thrives in indirect light, making it ideal for indoor spaces like living rooms or offices. The Peace Lily is not only beautiful but also helps purify the air. This plant is famous for adding a touch of nature and tranquility to any indoor setting.

The Peace Lily, known scientifically as Spathiphyllum wallisii, is a popular houseplant renowned for its lush, green foliage and white blooms. Spathiphyllum is derived from the Greek words: "spath" (spathe) and "phyllon" (leaf), referring to the leaf-like spathe that surrounds the flower spadix. Wallisii honors Gustav Wallis, the German plant collector who introduced many tropical plants to Europe. The Peace Lily was discovered in the late 19th century in Central and South American tropical rainforests. In modern times, the Peace Lily is often associated with peace, innocence, and purity. It's a popular choice for sympathy gifts and is often seen in offices and homes due to its air-purifying qualities.

CARING GUIDE

Water: Water regularly with filtered water, when the first inch the soil becomes dry, and keep its soil moderately moist.

Light: Prospers in areas not exposed to harsh to sun. Overexposure to strong sunlight can lead to scorched leaves, while underexposure can lead to slow growth.

Fertilization: Feeding every six weeks in the growing season is sufficient. Use a balanced, water-soluble houseplant fertilizer.

SUITABLE FOR:
Bedroom, Bathroom, Kitchen, Living Room, Office/Study Room, East or North-facing window

Prayer Plant
Maranta leuconeura (FAMILY: Marantaceae)

 **Light**
Ideal: Full Shade
Tolerate: Partial sun

 Water
Every Week

 Temparature
65-75°F
(18-24°C)

 Humidity
High
(60-70%)

 **Pets**
Safe for Cats and Dogs

Also known as: Rabbit Tracks, Herringbone Plant

The prayer plant, a dear resident in many homes, has a secret talent of coming alive at night; as the sun dips, its leaves rise gracefully, folding together like hands clasped in prayer. This daily ritual is how the plant catches the moonlight and dewdrops, keeping its thirsty self happy. This charmer prefers dappled light and a cozy humidity hug to flourish in your home.

Originating from the rainforests of Brazil, The Prayer Plant (Maranta leuconeura) is a captivating botanical wonder. The scientific name "Maranta" honors Bartolomeo Maranta, a 16th-century Venetian physician and botanist who made significant contributions to the field. He was known for his work on medicinal plants and published several influential books, including "Methodi cognoscendorum simplicium" (1559), which discussed medicinal herbs.

CARING GUIDE

Water: Water once a week in spring, summer, and fall, depending on weather, allowing the soil to dry between waterings.

Light: Thrives in environments with less illumination. Infrequent exposure to sunshine can be tolerated, yet extreme sunlight could be detrimental.

Fertilization: Fertilize prayer plant with a balanced, water-soluble fertilizer once every two weeks in spring, summer and fall.

SUITABLE FOR:
Bedroom, Bathroom, Kitchen, Living Room, Office/Study Room, Children's Room, East or North-facing window

"Leuconeura" comes from Greek, with "leuco" meaning white and "neura" meaning veins, referring to the plant's distinct leaf pattern. The Prayer Plant is often described as a living art piece because of its decorative leaves. Each leaf is like a unique painting, with patterns that can resemble brush strokes or splashes of paint. The most interesting feature of the Prayer Plant is the ability of its leaves to fold upward at night, a behavior known as nyctinasty. This movement is still not fully understood, but it's believed to be a way to reduce water loss and protect the plant from nocturnal pests. Research suggests that the Prayer Plant can also move its leaves in response to temperature changes, acting like a natural thermostat. The Prayer Plant's ability to fold and unfold its leaves has inspired both scientific curiosity and a sense of wonder. In the language of flowers, the Prayer Plant symbolizes gratitude and faithfulness.

Polka dot plant
Hypoestes phyllostachya (Family: Acanthaceae)

 Light	Water	 Temperature	Humidity	 Pets
Ideal: partial sun Tolerate: Full shade	Every Week	65-75°F (18-24°C)	High (60-80%)	Safe for Cats and Dogs

CARING GUIDE

Water: It requires frequent watering to keep the soil consistently moist. It's essential to avoid waterlogging the soil.

Light: Grows best in moderate light but can tolerate low light. Limited light may cause poor growth and faded colors, while too much light can damage its leaves.

Fertilization: Fertilize regularly during the growing season, in spring and fall. A balanced, houseplant fertilizer, is ideal.

SUITABLE FOR:
Bedroom, Bathroom, Kitchen, Living Room, Office/Study Room, East or North-facing window.

Also known as: Freckle Face, Measles Plant, Pink Splash

A commonly grown indoor plant is the Polka Dot Plant, recognizable for its variegated, spiky leaves decorated with colorful spots. It's most commonly found in pink, but there are also varieties with white and red hues. It's best to position this plant where it can receive bright, indirect sunlight. This optimal lighting enhances the vividness of its distinctively patterned foliage.

The Polka dot plant (Hypoestes phyllostachya) is native to Madagascar, South Africa, and southeast Asia. It was first documented in the 19th century and gained popularity in Victorian England as a decorative houseplant due to its vibrant foliage. The genus name "Hypoestes" is derived from Greek, where "hypo" means "under" and "estia" means "house". This could refer to the plant's growth habit, often under the canopy of larger plants in its native habitat. The specific epithet "Phyllostachya" comes from the Greek "phyllon," meaning "leaf," and "stachys," meaning "spike," referring to the plant's leafy spikes. The common name is quite literal, derived from the plant's distinctive polka dot-like pattern on its leaves.

Rabbit's Foot Fern

Davallia (Family: Davalliaceae)

 **Light**
Ideal: partial sun
Tolerate: full shade

 Water
Twice
per week

 Temperature
65-80°F
(18-27°C)

 Humidity
High
(60-70%)

 Pets
Safe for Cats
and Dogs

Also known as: Deer's Foot Fern, Squirrel's Foot Fern

Meet the fuzzy-footed charmer, the Rabbit's Foot Fern! This dainty fellow hangs out with other plants, absorbing the good stuff from the air with its feathery fronds. But its secret weapon? Tiny, furry roots that peek out like hobbit toes! Hang it up or plop it in a pot; just ensure it's warm, humid, and out of the sun's glare. Think jungle spa without the creepy crawlies.

The genus name, Davallia, is in honor of the 18th-century French botanist Edmond Davall. The common name "Rabbit's Foot Fern" is derived from the distinctive appearance of the plant's rhizomes, which are covered in fine, hair-like roots. These rhizomes resemble a rabbit's foot, especially when they cascade over the sides of a hanging basket or container. The rhizomes of the Rabbit's Foot Fern not only look interesting but also serve a purpose in nature. They allow the fern to "travel" as they spread over the soil surface and can root to form new plants. Besides "Rabbit's Foot Fern," it's also known as "Davallia," "Hare's Foot Fern," and "Squirrel Foot Fern," among others.

CARING GUIDE

Water: Water moderately, enough to make the soil moist. Allow the soil in the container to dry out slightly in between.

Light: Prefers areas exposed to moderate sunlight. This light intensity fosters healthy growth and development. It can withstand locations with limited light access.

Fertilization: Fertilization once in spring, or feed with a weak liquid fertilizer every 2-3 weeks throughout the growing season.

SUITABLE FOR:

Bedroom, Bathroom, Kitchen, Living Room, Office/Study Room, Children's Room, East or North-facing window

Rattlesnake Plant
Calathea lancifolia (Family: Marantaceae)

 Light	 Water	Temparature	Humidity	Pets
Ideal: Full Shade Tolerate: Partial sun	Every week	65-75°F (18-24°C)	High (60-70%)	Safe for Cats and Dogs

CARING GUIDE

Water: Will grow best in moist well-drained soil. Use distilled water, and do not leave it soaking in water for too long.

Light: Appreciates dimly lit locations and can endure a fair amount of sunlight exposure, but should be kept away from severe sun rays, which can lead to leaf burn.

Fertilization: Use a well-balanced, diluted to half balanced fertilizer every month, during spring and summer growing season..

SUITABLE FOR:
Bedroom, Bathroom, Kitchen, Living Room, Office/Study Room, Children's Room, East or North-facing window

Also known as: Rattlesnake ginger, Peacock plant

Meet the rattlesnake plant; this tropical stunner, the queen of the Goeppertia clan, practically begs to be your leafy companion. Its wavy stripes in shades of emerald will mesmerize you, and its care needs are as chill as a hammock under a palm tree. Just give it a warm spot, bright light that doesn't burn, and soil that's moist but not soaked, and it'll reward you with jungle vibes.

The genus name "Calathea" has its roots in Greek. It is derived from the Greek word "kalathos," which means "basket." This name was chosen due to the way the flowers were arranged, often resembling a basket. The intricate patterns and colors on the leaves of the Rattlesnake Plant can symbolize elegance and grace. Its unique foliage adds aesthetic beauty to indoor spaces. The name "Rattlesnake Plant" for Calathea lancifolia likely comes from the distinctive markings on its leaves resembling the rattlesnake's skin pattern. The elongated, lance-shaped leaves of the plant have a striking and intricate design with wavy lines and contrasting colors, much like the markings on a rattlesnake.

RUBBER PLANT
Ficus elastica (Family: Moraceae)

LIGHT	WATER	TEMPERATURE	HUMIDITY	PETS
Ideal: Partial sun Tolerate: Full sun, Full shade	Every 1-2 weeks	60-75°F (15-24°C)	Moderate (40-50%)	Not Safe for Cats and Dogs

Also known as: Rubber Fig, Rubber Tree, Rubber Bush

Meet the rubber tree, a glossy giant with a secret past! This leafy legend boasts wide, oval leaves that gleam like polished emeralds. But did you know its milky sap was once used to make rubber before that rainforest superstar, the Pará rubber tree, stole the spotlight? This beauty is all about brightening homes in cooler climates, bringing a touch of tropical magic to any room.

The Rubber Plant (Ficus elastica) is native to eastern South Asia and Southeast Asia. The genus "Ficus" is Latin for fig, a genus of about 850 species of woody trees, shrubs, vines, epiphytes, and hemiepiphytes. The epithet "Elastica" refers to the elastic properties of the rubber produced from the plant. While it's called the Rubber Plant, its commercial use for producing rubber was short-lived. It was one of the earliest sources of natural rubber until the more efficient Hevea brasiliensis took over the rubber industry. The Ficus genus, to which the Rubber Plant belongs, is ancient and was around during the time of the dinosaurs. This makes the Rubber Plant a living piece of history.

CARING GUIDE

Water: Water regularly with room temp. water, and let the soil dry in between. Dry periods are better than overwatering.

Light: Prefers a balance sunlight, thriving in a situation where it receives equal light and shadow. Originating from an environment of mixed light levels.

Fertilization: Prefers fertilization with a balanced, water-soluble standard fertilizer, every few weeks during spring and fall.

SUITABLE FOR:
Bedroom, Kitchen, Living Room, Balcony/Patio, South or West-facing window

SATIN POTHOS
Scindapsus pictus (Family: Araceae)

LIGHT	WATER	TEMPARATURE	HUMIDITY	 PETS
Ideal: Full Shade Tolerate: Partial sun	Every Week	65-75°F (18-24°C)	Moderate (40-60%)	Not Safe for Cats and Dogs

CARING GUIDE

Water: Water once a week whenever the top inch of soil dries out. Be sure the water drains thoroughly to prevent root rot.

Light: Prefers filtered or diminished sunlight, often found thriving in shadow, forest-like habitats. Sufficient exposure to the sun is essential for healthy growth.

Fertilization: Feed with half-strength balanced, water-soluble fertilizer once every four weeks during the spring and summer only.

SUITABLE FOR:
Bedroom, Bathroom, Kitchen, Living Room, Office/Study Room, East or North-facing window

Also known as: Silk Pothos, Silver Vine, Scindapsus

Hailing from the balmy tropics of Bangladesh, Thailand, Malaysia, Borneo, and the Philippines, the satin pothos have found a welcome in our living spaces as a beloved houseplant. It has many variations under the Scindapsus name; all have different patterns and markings. The thick green leaves and silvery patches are distinguishing features that all share.

Satin Pothos, scientifically known as Scindapsus pictus, is native to Southeast Asia and the western Pacific. The genus name "Scindapsus" is derived from the Greek words "skindapsos," which is thought to refer to some ivy-like plants, highlighting the resemblance of its leaves and growth form to ivy. The term "pothos" has its origins in ancient Greek. The word is associated with desire, longing, or passionate yearning. In the context of plants, the term "Pothos" is commonly used as a generic name for various vining plants within the Araceae family. This usage likely reflects the plants' vigorous growth and the desire of gardeners to have fast-growing, attractive vines in their indoor or outdoor spaces.

SPIDER PLANT
Chlorophytum comosum (FAMILY: Asparagaceae)

☀ LIGHT	💧 WATER	🌡 TEMPERATURE	💧 HUMIDITY	🐾 PETS
Ideal: Partial sun Tolerate: Full shade	Every Week	60-80°F (15-27°C)	Moderate (40-60%)	Safe for Cats and Dogs

Also known as: Airplane Plant, St. Bernard's Lily

This easygoing greenie, known as the spider plant, is a champion of long, flowing leaves that earned it another nickname: the ribbon plant. Originally from Africa, thanks to its chill vibes and low maintenance, it's a globe-trotting houseplant superstar. It just unfurls its graceful ribbons, gracefully spreads its long, thin leaves, and brings a touch of carefree nature indoors.

Spider Plant, also known as Chlorophytum comosum, is native to tropical and southern Africa. It was first discovered in the 9th century. The name "Chlorophytum" comes from the Greek words "chloros," meaning "green," and "phyton," meaning "plant." Spider Plant is also known as "airplane plant" because of its arching leaves that resemble airplane wings. The plant is known for its effectiveness in removing harmful toxins such as formaldehyde, carbon monoxide, and xylene from the air. Spider Plant was first formally described by the Swedish naturalist Carl Peter Thunberg in 794, who called it Anthericum comosum, considering it a close relative of St. Bernard's lily (A liliago), southern Europe's "spider plant."

CARING GUIDE

Water: Allow partial but not total soil drying between waterings. Brown tips? Deep water in a draining pot to flush salts.

Light: Prefers moderate sunlight. Too much sun might damage it, while too little could stunt its growth. This plant is resilient and can adapt to low light conditions.

Fertilization: Use a commercial all-purpose fertilizer no more frequently than every two weeks during the growing season.

SUITABLE FOR:
Bedroom, Bathroom, Kitchen, Living Room, Office/Study Room, Balcony/Patio, East or North-facing window

Snake Plant
Sansevieria trifasciata (FAMILY: Asparagaceae)

☼ LIGHT	💧 WATER	🌡 TEMPARATURE	% HUMIDITY	🔪 PETS
Ideal: Partial sun Tolerate: Full sun, Full shade	Every 3 weeks	60-80°F (15-27°C)	Moderate (40-60%)	Not Safe for Cats and Dogs

Also known as: Mother-in-Law's Tongue, Devil's Tongue

The low-maintenance superhero of the houseplant world. Stiff and sword-like leaves may sound intimidating, but this beauty is actually a gentle giant, happy to thrive in the shade and forget the occasional watering. It comes in a dazzling array of green stripes and creamy borders, making it the perfect pop of graphic elegance for your office or any space that needs a touch of quiet drama.

The Snake Plant (Sansevieria trifasciata) is native to West Africa, specifically Nigeria and the Congo. The genus name "Sansevieria" refers to Raimondo di Sangro, Prince of San Severo, an 18th-century Italian inventor, soldier, and nobleman. The genus Sansevieria honors his contributions to horticulture. "Trifasciata" is derived from Latin, meaning "three-banded" or "three-striped," referring to the plant's patterned leaves. Another common name

CARING GUIDE

Water: Grows best if its soil dries out completely in between waterings. Overwatering is the most common faced mistake.

Light: Thrives effectively under scattered sunlight, tolerating both fully-shaded and exposed conditions. It's known for its adaptability to various light conditions.

Fertilization: Should avoid overfertilization. If preferred, all-purpose houseplant food once a year in the spring is sufficent.

SUITABLE FOR:
Bedroom, Bathroom, Kitchen, Living Room, Office/Study Room, Balcony/Patio, East or North-facing window

for the Snake Plant is Mother-in-law's Tongue; this name is likely derived from the sharp, pointed leaves, which may resemble a mother-in-law's pointed and sometimes sharp-tongued nature. The plant is also commonly named "Saint George's Sword." This name is derived from the legendary figure Saint George, a Roman soldier revered as a Christian martyr. Saint George is most known for the myth of Saint George and the Dragon, where he is depicted slaying a dragon, often with a sword. The long, upright, and pointed leaves of the Snake Plant resemble a sword, drawing a parallel to the sword of Saint George in the legend. Historically, the Snake Plant was used for fiber production. The plant's strong fibers were used to make bowstrings, hence another common name, "Bowstring Hemp." Furthermore, in traditional African medicine, it has been used for various purposes, including as an antiseptic in wound healing.

Watermelon Peperomia
Peperomia argyreia (Family: Piperaceae)

Light	Water	Temperature	Humidity	Pets
Ideal: full shade Tolerate: partial sun	Every Week	65-75°F (18-24°C)	Moderate (50-60%)	Safe for Cats and Dogs

CARING GUIDE

Water: Needs deep watering. You need to make sure there is enough to penetrate deeply and the roots are completely soaked.

Light: Watermelon peperomia is a plant that thrives in areas where the sun do not reach in full intensity. It can also endure a certain degree of sun exposure.

Fertilization: Too much will cause weak, leggy growth. Use a liquid fertilizer (one-quarter strength) once a month, Spring-Summer.

SUITABLE FOR:
Bedroom, Bathroom, Kitchen, Living Room, Office/Study Room, Children's Room, East or North-facing window

Also known as: Watermelon pepper, Peperomia Sandersii

Watermelon peperomia (Peperomia argyreia) have become popular among houseplant lovers thanks to their stunning watermelon-patterned foliage. This tropical cutie's is an easygoing plant that even beginners can master. Its leaves, striped like a watermelon's rind, hint at its playful personality. Just give it a spot out of direct sun and soil that drains well, and it'll thrive.

The earliest documented mention of the Watermelon Peperomia appears in 1854, when Eduard Morren, a Belgian botanist, coined its scientific name "Peperomia argyreia." This suggests the plant was already known and potentially cultivated before then. The decorative Watermelon peperomia gets its common name from the distinctive watermelon-like stripes on its foliage. Its scientific name, Peperomia argyreia, comes from Greek, Peperomia referring to pepper-like plants, and argyreia meaning silvery. This tropical perennial plant hails from the rainforests of Ecuador and Peru in South America, where the indigenous communities living in the rainforests likely held knowledge about the plant long before its scientific discovery.

WAX PLANT
Hoya carnosa (Family: Apocynaceae)

LIGHT
Ideal: Partial sun
Tolerate: Full shade

WATER
Every
3 weeks

TEMPARATURE
60-75°F
(15-24°C)

HUMIDITY
Moderate
(40-50%)

PETS
Safe for Cats
and Dogs

Also known as: Porcelain Flower, Hindu Rope Plant

This little charmer, the porcelainflower, hails from East Asia and Australia. This houseplant pro is a breath of fresh air, literally. It's known for its knack of sucking up indoor toxins, making your home a healthier haven. And that's not all! The porcelain flower boasts a sweet nectar that lures in friendly pollinators, adding a touch of buzzing magic to your space.

Its common name, "Wax Plant," is a nod to its thick, glossy leaves that resemble polished wax. The nickname "Porcelain flower," on the other hand, is a tribute to its delicate star-shaped blooms that possess a porcelain-like texture. The Hoya Carnosa plant was named after Thomas Hoy, a British botanist who brought attention to Hoyas. The specific epithet "carnosa" refers to the fleshy texture of its leaves. In China, the Wax Plant is revered for its association with luck and prosperity. It is often gifted during Chinese New Year celebrations, symbolizing good fortune and abundance for the year ahead. In Thailand, the plant is believed to promote love and fidelity, making it a popular choice for wedding gifts.

CARING GUIDE

Water: Let it dry out between watering. Soak the soil until drainage. The more light, the more water, adjust as needed.

Light: Prefers environments with moderate sunshine and a fair quantity of shade. Lack of exposure may stunt growth, while excessive exposure can cause foliage damage.

Fertilization: Feed Hoya carnosa with a high nitrogen fertilizer once a month. A 3-1-2 or 2-1-2 liquid fertilizer is recommended.

SUITABLE FOR:
Bedroom, Bathroom, Kitchen, Living Room, Office/Study Room, East or North-facing window

Weeping Fig
Ficus benjamina (Family: Moraceae)

Light	Water	Temparature	Humidity	Pets
Ideal: Partial sun Tolerate: Full sun, Full shade	Every 1-2 weeks	65-80°F (18-27°C)	High (60-80%)	Not Safe for Cats and Dogs

CARING GUIDE

Water: Water regularly between spring and fall during the growing season. Overwatering it can cause the leaves to drop.

Light: Prefers to grow in a location where it is exposed to light for some of the day but also enjoys occasional shade. Borne in a habitat where light levels fluctuate.

Fertilization: Needs balanced 10-10-10 fertilizer once a month at least during the active growing season between spring and fall.

SUITABLE FOR: Living Room, South or West-facing window

Also known as: Benjamin Fig, Ficus Tree, Weeping Fig Tree

The weeping fig, a native of Asia and Australia, is an authentic, captivating houseplant. Its slender cascading branches with glossy leaves have stolen hearts around the world. This beauty, while harmless to nibble on (except for the fruit, which is a bonus treat), packs a sneaky punch in the form of indoor allergens. So, if you are allergic, it might be best to admire this charmer from afar.

The common name "Weeping Fig" derives from its appearance. This plant has drooping branches and leaves, giving it a "weeping" look. Ficus benjamina is native to Asia and Australia and is the official tree of Bangkok. It's also naturalized in the West Indies, Florida, and Arizona in the United States. The Ficus genus, to which Ficus benjamina belongs, is sometimes mentioned in cultural and religious contexts. It is considered holy in East Asia as Buddha gained enlightenment under a fig tree. In Indonesia, it is believed that weeping figs are the link between the human and spirit worlds. In some cultures, the Ficus benjamina is considered a symbol of protection, prosperity, and good luck.

ZZ Plant
Zamioculcas zamiifolia (Family: Araceae)

LIGHT	**WATER**	**TEMPERATURE**	**HUMIDITY**	**PETS**
Ideal: Partial sun Tolerate: Full shade	Every 3 weeks	60-80°F (15-27°C)	Moderate (40-60%)	Not Safe for Cats and Dogs

Also known as: Zanzibar Gem, Eternity Plant, Aroid Palm

The ZZ Plant is a sturdy plant from Eastern Africa that has become a favorite all over the world because it's so easy to take care of. It's a great plant to have in the house because it doesn't need much light or water to thrive. People sometimes call it the "Zanzibar Gem" because its smooth, shiny leaves start off a bright lime color and turn a deep green as they grow.

The ZZ Plant, scientifically known as Zamioculcas zamiifolia, is a tropical perennial plant native to Eastern Africa. The meaning of the specific epithet "zamiifolia" is "leaves like Zamia." This refers to the similarity of the structure of the leaves of this plant to the leaves of the members of the genus Zamia. The genus name "Zamioculcas" comes from a combination of two terms, "Zamia," which is a genus of cycad due to the superficial resemblance in leaf appearance, and "culcas," an Arabic name for the colocasia plant. Interestingly, the ZZ Plant is believed to have prehistoric origins. Its structure and growth patterns are thought to be similar to ancient plants, making it a living piece of botanical history.

CARING GUIDE

Water: Should be allowed to dry out completely in between watering and to never sit in stagnant water, as roots will rot.

Light: Thrives in areas with a fair amount of sunlight, and it's quite tolerant of more shaded locations. Its habitat is typically regions with filtered light.

Fertilization: Fertilized once a month with a well-balanced houseplant diluted liquid fertilizer, with a 20-20-20 formulation.

SUITABLE FOR:
Bedroom, Bathroom, Kitchen, Living Room, Office/Study Room, East or North-facing window

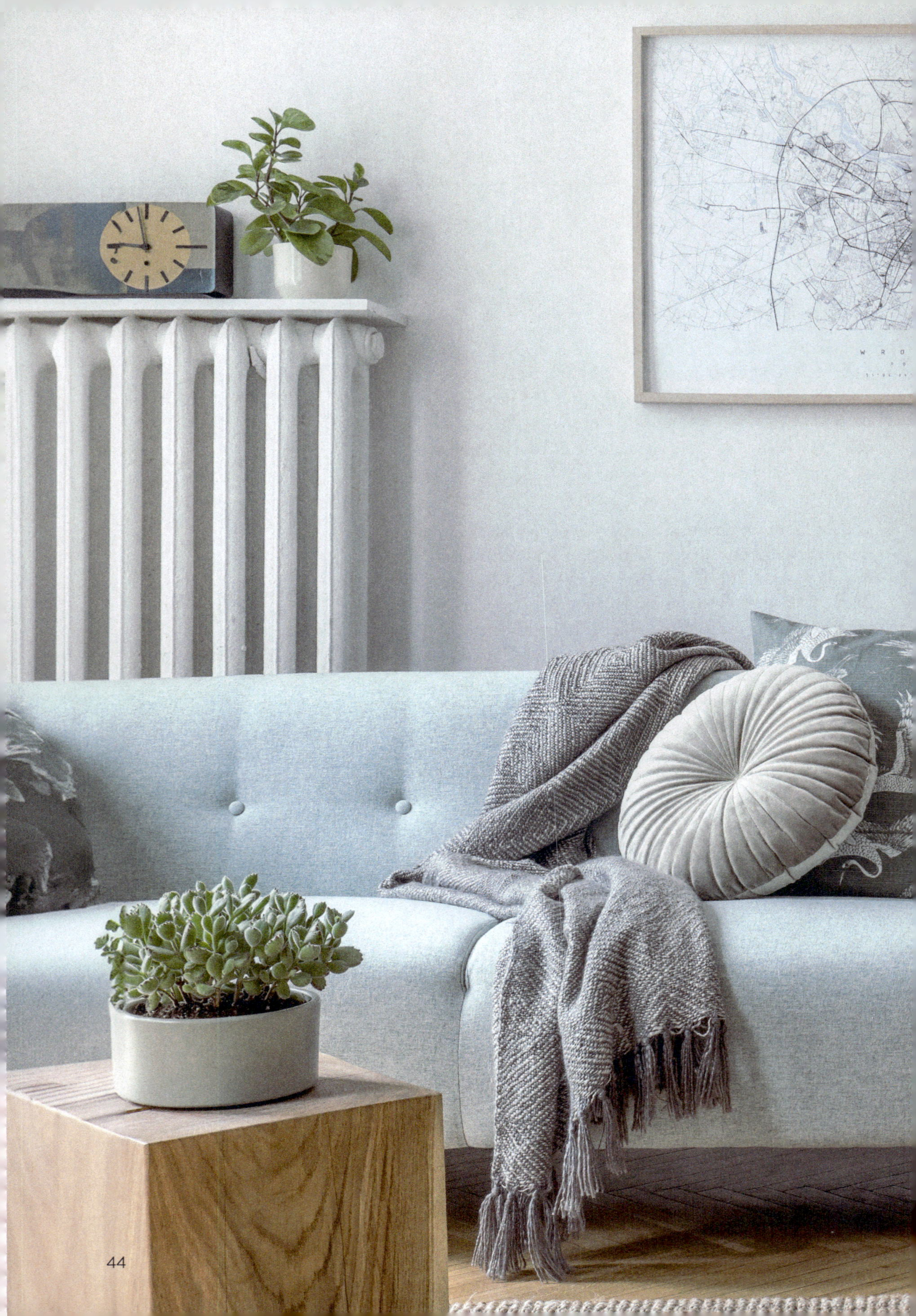

Section 2:
MEDIUM LIGHT PLANTS

Bathed in Soft Light: A Guide to Medium Light Plants

This book section focuses on medium-light plants, ideal for places with indirect sunlight. It includes a variety of plants, suitable for areas with moderate light. The guide offers practical advice on placement, watering, and care, making these plants an easy and attractive choice for indoor gardening. These medium-light plants are adaptable and can enhance any space with their presence.

African Violet
Saintpaulia ionantha (FAMILY: Gesneriaceae)

LIGHT	WATER	TEMPARATURE	HUMIDITY	PETS
Ideal: Partial sun	Every Week	65-80°F (18-27°C)	High (60-80%)	Safe for Cats and Dogs
Tolerate: Full shade				

CARING GUIDE

Water: Water weekly on average, by immersing the pot in slightly warm water up to the soil line, then letting it drain.

Light: Prefers moderate sunlight, seen in its native forest environment. Too much illumination can lead to leaf scorching, whereas a lack of light may hinder blooms.

Fertilization: Fertilize once a month with a well-balanced 14-12-14 fertilizer while the plant is only in the blooming period.

SUITABLE FOR:
Bedroom, Bathroom, Kitchen, Living Room, Children's Room, East or North-facing window

Also known as: Saintpaulia, Usambara Violet, African Violet

This little plant is well-loved for its adorable and charming appearance. It's no wonder it's a household favorite. Its compact size and those cheery blooms in blue, pink, purple, or white brighten up any corner! This beauty practically blooms all year round, but it's a bit of a diva regarding the cold. Keep it at 55 °F or warmer; it'll shower you with endless flower power!

African Violets (Saintpaulia ionantha) are native to the cloud forests of Tanzania and Kenya. The name "African Violet" is derived from its resemblance to true violets (genus Viola) and its origin in East Africa. The genus name "Saintpaulia" honors Baron Walter von Saint Paul-Illaire, who first discovered the plant in Tanzania in 1892. The species name "ionantha" comes from Greek, meaning "violet flower.". After its discovery, Baron Walter sent specimens to his father in Germany, which sparked interest among European botanists and horticulturists. African Violets were one of the first plants to be grown in space. NASA used them during the 1970s in the Skylab program to study the effects of zero gravity on plants.

ALOCASIA
Alocasia spp. (Family: Araceae)

LIGHT
Ideal: Partial sun
Tolerate: Full shade

WATER
Every Week

TEMPERATURE
65-75°F
(18-24°C)

HUMIDITY
High
(60-80%)

PETS
Not Safe for Cats and Dogs

Also known as: Elephant Ear, African Mask Plant, Kris Plant

With leaves so grand, they resemble an elephant's ears. That's the Elephant Ear plant, a hybrid of two Alocasia species. Native to the lush tropics of Asia and Australia, this beauty is renowned for its dramatic foliage, with leaves that can reach up to 3 feet in length. Each leaf is a masterpiece of nature's artistry; its deep green surface resembles a delicate network of lace.

Alocasia earned its colloquial name, "Elephant Ear," due to the shape and size of its distinctive leaves. These oversized, heart-shaped leaves bear an uncanny resemblance to the ears of an elephant. Early botanical texts in the 18th and 19th centuries used the term "Colocasia" to refer to several similar genera. However, around the 1830s, "Alocasia" emerged as a distinct genus name, likely to differentiate it from other Colocasia species. The alteration could have been to emphasize the edible nature of the plant's root, as the "a-" prefix in Greek can sometimes have the meaning of "without" or "not," suggesting the absence of the bitterness associated with some "Colocasia" species.

CARING GUIDE

Water: Prefers once a week when the soil surface dries out. Water thoroughly until saturation and drain the excess water.

Light: Loves moderate sunlight, and can survive in relatively devoid of light. Thrives more when akin to its natural habitat where the sun isn't overly concentrated.

Fertilization: Fertilizer is not necessary. Can be met by repotting into a larger pot of fresh, good-quality soil once yearly.

SUITABLE FOR:
Bathroom, East or North-facing window

ALOE VERA
Aloe vera (FAMILY: Asphodelaceae)

☀️ LIGHT	💧 WATER	🌡️ TEMPERATURE	💧 HUMIDITY	🐾 PETS
Ideal: Partial sun Tolerate: Full sun, Full shade	Every 3 weeks	65-80°F (18-27°C)	Low (20-40%)	Not Safe for Cats and Dogs

Also known as: Chinese aloe, Wand of heaven, Burn aloe

The Aloe vera is a true survivor emerging from the sun-scorched Arabian Peninsula. Its thick leaves are nature's water bottles, storing moisture to endure the harsh desert conditions. This resilient succulent has found a new home in our homes, adding a touch of greenery to our lives. Aloe vera's flesh is a treasure trove of healing properties, gracing our skin with its soothing touch.

The name "Aloe vera" combines Arabic and Latin origins. "Aloe" comes from the Arabic "Alloeh," meaning "shining bitter substance." The Latin word "vera" means "true," distinguishing Aloe vera from other species in the Aloe genus due to its perceived effectiveness. Historically, Aloe vera was important in ancient Egyptian culture. They called it the "plant of immortality," and it was a funeral gift to pharaohs. This is evident in the Ebers Papyrus, an ancient Egyptian

CARING GUIDE

Water: Top third of the potting soil should dry out before watering. Watered twice as frequently in spring as in winter.

Light: Thrives under moderate sun exposure, and can tolerate intense or minimal sunlight; an adaptation from its native habitat

Fertilization: Does not need fertilization. Once a year with a water-soluble fertilizer (containing phosphorous) is sufficient.

SUITABLE FOR: Bedroom, Kitchen, Living Room, Office/Study Room, Balcony/Patio, South or West-facing window

medical document, where Aloe vera is mentioned for its laxative properties and as a treatment for skin conditions. Aloe vera was also a common ingredient in various beauty preparations. Cleopatra and Nefertiti, the renowned beauties of ancient Egypt, are believed to have used Aloe vera as part of their skincare routines. The plant's medicinal value was recognized by others, including Alexander the Great. Reportedly advised by Aristotle, he captured the island of Socotra to access its Aloe vera resources, ensuring a supply for treating his soldiers' wounds. Aloe vera has also been used in various cultures for spiritual purposes, such as warding off evil spirits. Originally from the Arabian Peninsula, it is now grown worldwide, especially in tropical climates. The plant is known for its durability, living up to 12 years under proper care. This resilience is largely due to its ability to store water in its leaves, which helps it survive in dry conditions.

Areca Palm
Dypsis lutescens (Family: Arecaceae)

Light	**Water**	**Temperature**	**Humidity**	**Pets**
Ideal: Partial sun Tolerate: Full sun, Full shade	Every 1-2 weeks	65-80°F (18-27°C)	Moderate (50-60%)	Safe for Cats and Dogs

CARING GUIDE

Water: Thrives in moist soils during the warmer seasons, so water it regularly, without waterlogging to avoid root rot.

Light: Prefers a balance between sun and shade, tolerating varied lighting conditions as long as there's adequate daylight, and thrives even without excessive light.

Fertilization: Use a well-diluted and if you aren't sure then use less fertilizer. Fertilize monthly during the growing season.

SUITABLE FOR:
Bedroom, Bathroom, Kitchen, Living Room, Balcony/Patio, Children's Room, East or North-facing window

Also known as: Butterfly Palm, Golden Cane Palm

Meet the butterfly palm, a sunshine-loving beauty straight out of Madagascar! Some call it the golden cane palm, others the yellow palm, but this leafy charmer just loves to soak up the limelight. It basks in the sun in tropical paradises as a gorgeous outdoor star. But in cooler climates like ours, it brings a touch of island magic indoors, becoming the envy of all your houseplant pals.

The Areca Palm, scientifically known as Dypsis lutescens, is native to Madagascar. The genus name "Areca" is believed to come from the Dravidian term "aṯ-ay-kkāy," which translates to "areca nut" in Malayalam, a language spoken in the region. The epithet "lutescens" is Latin for "growing yellow," referring to this palm's yellow petioles or stems. It's commonly known as golden cane palm, areca palm, yellow palm, butterfly palm, or bamboo palm. These names often allude to its physical characteristics, like its golden color or resemblance to Bamboo. In its native Madagascar, various parts of the plant may have been used in traditional practices or as material for crafting items such as baskets and mats.

Cape Primrose
Streptocarpus spp. (Family: Gesneriaceae)

LIGHT	**WATER**	**TEMPARATURE**	**HUMIDITY**	**PETS**
Ideal: Partial sun Tolerate: Full shade	Every Week	55-70°F (13-21°C)	Moderate (50-60%)	Safe for Cats and Dogs

Also known as: False African Violet, Streptocarpella

If you love the look of African violets but find them too difficult to grow, try a pot of their hardier cousins, the cape primrose. Streptocarpus plants are often recommended as a practice exercise for growing African violets. This is because the two species share similar requirements, but Cape primrose is hardier. The Cape primrose flowers resemble African violets with their hues of pink, purple, and white.

The name "Streptocarpus" is derived from the Greek words "streptos" meaning twisted or curved, and "karpos" meaning fruit. The name refers to the unique twisted seed capsules that develop after the flowers have bloomed. As for the common name "Cape Primrose," it likely originates from the plant's native region and its visual resemblance to Primula species, which are commonly known as primroses. The "Cape" in the name might refer to the Cape Floristic Region in South Africa, where many Streptocarpus species are found. The tubular flowers of Streptocarpus are designed to attract pollinators like hummingbirds in their native habitats. This adaptation is reflected in the plant's tubular and often brightly colored flowers.

CARING GUIDE

Water: Requires regular watering. Water once a week on average, adjusting based on the temperature and humidity levels.

Light: Loves light but direct sunlight can burn its foliage. A home with an east or west-facing window is perfect for it, but if a southern you can add a sheer curtain.

Fertilization: Fertilize during spring and summer, every two weeks with a balanced liquid fertilizer diluted to half strength.

SUITABLE FOR:
Bedroom, Kitchen, Living Room, Children's Room, East or North-facing window

Common Staghorn Fern

Platycerium bifurcatum (Family: Polypodiaceae)

LIGHT	**WATER**	**TEMPARATURE**	**HUMIDITY**	**PETS**
Ideal: Partial sun	Every	65-80°F	High	Safe for Cats
Tolerate: Full shade	Week	(18-27°C)	(60-70%)	and Dogs

CARING GUIDE

Water: Needs to be both misted and watered. Water by soaking the root ball in a bucket and drip-drying before rehanging.

Light: In its native habitat, it experiences filtered sunlight but can also thrive in less sun exposure areas. However, exposure to too much sun can harm its health.

Fertilization: Fertilized during the growing season twice a year. A balanced liquid diluted feed is ideally to prevent burning.

SUITABLE FOR:

Bedroom, Bathroom, Kitchen, Living Room, Children's Room, East or North-facing window

Also known as: Elk's Horn Fern, Staghorn Fern

Meet the staghorn fern, a plant with a serious attitude! Instead of roots in the soil, it hitches a ride on other things. It even has antlers! Well, not antlers exactly, but spiky green fronds that can grow up to three feet long indoors. And below, it hides little round shields that protect its roots. This fern's definitely not your average houseplant, but that's what makes it so special.

The Common Staghorn Fern (Platycerium bifurcatum) is native to the rainforests of New Guinea and southeastern Australia. The genus name "Platycerium" is derived from the Greek words platys, meaning "flat," and ceras, meaning "horn." This is in reference to the plant's fertile fronds resembling a flat horn. The specific epithet bifurcatum means bifurcated or forked, again referring to the shape of the fertile fronds. Staghorn Ferns are epiphytic, meaning they grow on other surfaces, such as trees or rocks. However, they don't take nutrients from the host; instead, they absorb water and nutrients from the air and rain. The cup-shaped base of the fern acts as a natural reservoir that collects rainwater.

CROTON
Codiaeum variegatum (Family: Euphorbiaceae)

☀ LIGHT	💧 WATER	🌡 TEMPARATURE	💧 HUMIDITY	🧪 PETS
Ideal: Partial sun Tolerate: full sun	Every 1-2 weeks	65-80°F (18-27°C)	Moderate (50-60%)	Not Safe for Cats and Dogs

Also known as: Joseph's Coat, Garden Croton

The garden croton is like a party for your eyes, exploding with color and personality. This indoor-outdoor chameleon rock leaves come in every shade from fiery orange to sunshine yellow, fabulous emerald to shocking scarlet, sometimes all on the same plant! It is guaranteed to jazz up your home or warm-weather patio. Plus, its unique shapes and textures add a touch of sculptural flair.

Croton (Codiaeum variegatum) is native to Southeast Asia and the Pacific Islands. The genus name "Croton" comes from the Greek word "kroton," which means "tick." This name likely refers to the shape of the seeds of some Croton species. The name Codiaeum variegatum reflects its diverse leaf patterns and colors. The Croton genus is ancient and diverse, with over 1,000 species. While Codiaeum variegatum is the most famous, its cousins include plants with a wide array of uses, from industrial (like the oil-producing Croton tiglium) to purely ornamental. In some cultures, the Croton plant is seen as a symbol of endurance and perseverance due to its resilient nature and ability to thrive in varying environmental conditions.

CARING GUIDE

Water: The garden croton's soil must be kept slightly moist at all times during the growing season from spring to summer.

Light: Prefers a balance of sunlight and shade, and able tolerate extended periods of sun exposure. Its lush growth is conspicuously supported by filtered sunlight.

Fertilization: Apply a liquid acidifying fertilizers reduced to half-strength every other month, during the active growing season.

SUITABLE FOR: Living Room, Balcony/Patio, East or North-facing window

Flame Violet

Episcia cupreata (Family: Gesneriaceae)

LIGHT
Ideal: partial sun
Tolerate: full shade

WATER
Every week

TEMPERATURE
65-75°F
(18-24°C)

HUMIDITY
High
(60-70%)

PETS
Safe for Cats and Dogs

CARING GUIDE

Water: Water regularly to keep soil evenly moist spring through fall. Keep slightly drier in winter when growth is slowed.

Light: Prefers moderate sunlight, while being adaptable to areas with less light. Sunlight influences its healthy growth, though too much can harm its delicate leaves.

Fertilization: Fertilize your Flame Violet plant every 2 weeks spring through fall (no winter), with African violet fertilizer.

SUITABLE FOR:

Bedroom, Bathroom, Kitchen, Living Room, Office/Study Room, Children's Room, East or North-facing window

Also known as: Trailing Flame Violet, Copper Violet

Meet the flame violet; this cutie's not just about the stunning, fire-kissed flowers - its leaves are a mosaic of emerald and copper, like a tiny autumn forest. It loves to crawl and trail, making it perfect for hanging baskets and pots or even taking over a corner as ground cover. Think of it as a tiny jungle explorer, always seeking new horizons (maybe a sunbeam or two).

The Flame Violet (Episcia cupreata) was discovered in Colombia in 1845 by a collector from Kew, W. M Purdie. He spotted a plant and asked that seeds be sent to him when they ripened. In 1847, the red-flowered plants bloomed and were identified as a new species. It quickly made its way into the garden trade in Europe and England. The genus name, Episcia, comes from the Greek word "episkios," meaning shady. This is likely a reference to the plant's natural habitat, often found growing in the shaded understory of tropical forests. The species name, cupreata, is derived from the Latin word "cupreus," meaning copper. This refers to the copper or bronze coloration often found in the foliage of Flame Violets.

FLAMINGO FLOWER
Anthurium andraeanum (Family: Araceae)

☀ LIGHT	💧 WATER	🌡 TEMPERATURE	💧 HUMIDITY	🧪 PETS
Ideal: Partial sun Tolerate: Full Shade	Every Week	65-80°F (18-27°C)	High (60-80%)	Not Safe for Cats and Dogs

Also known as: Painter's-palette, Oilcloth flower

The flamingo flower, renowned for its exotic and ornamental appeal, is a captivating perennial plant celebrated for its vibrant heart-shaped blooms in pink or fiery red shades. These blossoms, complemented by prominent pistils, introduce a touch of tropical elegance to any setting. Beyond its decorative charm, the flamingo flower has remarkable air-purifying properties.

The Flamingo Flower, scientifically known as Anthurium andraeanum, is a striking and popular houseplant known for its distinctive, heart-shaped flowers. Its common name, "Flamingo Flower," is derived from the plant's resemblance to the bright pink or red color of a flamingo's feathers. The scientific name "Anthurium" comes from the Greek words "anthos," meaning "flower," and "oura," meaning "tail," referring to the tail-like spadix. "Andraeanum" is likely a homage to Édouard André, a French horticulturist and explorer who discovered it in Colombia and introduced it to Europe in the late 19th century. Anthurium andraeanum is seen as a symbol of hospitality and is used in floral arrangements to convey this sentiment.

CARING GUIDE

Water: Water infrequently, but thoroughly during the active growing season. Let the soil dry slightly between waterings.

Light: Thrives in protected from heavy sun areas. With its origin in the shadowy tropical forests, it can also handle periods of lighter sun conditions.

Fertilization: Fertilize bi-monthly during spring and fall. A diluted to one-fourth, balanced, water-soluble fertilizer is ideal.

SUITABLE FOR:
Bedroom, Bathroom, Living Room, South or West-facing window

FRIENDSHIP PLANT

Pilea involucrata (FAMILY: Urticaceae)

LIGHT	WATER	TEMPARATURE	HUMIDITY	PETS
Ideal: Partial sun Tolerate: Full shade	Every Week	65-75°F (18-24°C)	Moderate (40-50%)	Safe for Cats and Dogs

CARING GUIDE

Water: Does not like to dry out. So, water it regularly, and avoid overwatering that leads to soggy soil and root rot.

Light: Keep It out of the direct sun, as this will burn the leaves. It prefers bright indirect light. A kitchen counter with a south or west-facing window works well.

Fertilization: Fertilize once a month during the spring and summer with an all purpose liquid balanced, half-strength fertilizer

SUITABLE FOR:
Bedroom, Bathroom, Kitchen, Living Room, Office/Study Room, Children's Room, East or North-facing window

Also known as: Panamiga

Have you ever heard of a plant that practically radiates friendship? Well, meet Pilea involucrata, the actual deal friendship plant. This disco-ball beauty flaunts textured leaves that shimmer bronze and silver, like a tiny party favor you can keep forever. Plus, its opposite, oval leaves and unique coloring make it stand. This plant deserves a spot in your life (and your next Instagram post).

The common name "Friendship Plant" is likely linked to the plant's natural inclination to generate offsets or "pups," facilitating effortless propagation and the opportunity to share it with friends. The name of the Friendship Plant inherently implies a connection to camaraderie and the notion of exchanging plants as a symbol of friendship. Beyond its symbolic significance, Pilea involucrata has historical applications in traditional medicine, where it has been utilized to address a spectrum of health concerns, ranging from respiratory issues and skin conditions to digestive ailments. The leaves of this plant are traditionally believed to harbor a diverse array of anti-inflammatory and antimicrobial properties.

GLOXINIA
Sinningia speciosa (Family: Gesneriaceae)

LIGHT	WATER	TEMPERATURE	HUMIDITY	PETS
Ideal: Partial sun Tolerate: full sun	Twice per week	65-75°F (18-24°C)	Moderate (50-60%)	Safe for Cats and Dogs

Also known as: Sinningia, Florist's Gloxinia

Gloxinia is the velvet-leafed diva with a floral crown. This summertime showstopper reaches for the sun and rewards you with the most stunning, bell-shaped blooms in blue, purple, pink, red, and white. It attracts hummingbirds and butterflies, so your porch might become a magical buzzing oasis. This beauty is usually a houseplant queen but loves outdoor summer strolls.

Gloxinia, scientifically known as Sinningia speciosa, is native to Brazil and is a member of the family Gesneriaceae. The genus "Sinningia" is named after Wilhelm Sinning, the head gardener at the University of Bonn. The species name "speciosa" translates to "showy" or "good-looking. This term is frequently used in scientific naming to describe organisms with impressive features. The plant was sent to England from Brazil in 1815 and first published and illustrated by the English nurseryman Conrad Loddiges in 1817 as Gloxinia speciosa. English travelers took the plant to colonial settlements, reaching places like Mauritius, India, Barbados, the British Virgin Islands, and Sri Lanka throughout the 19th century.

CARING GUIDE

Water: Water regularly when the top 3 cm of soil has dries, keep soil moist, and avoid overwatering to prevent root rot.

Light: Gloxinia requires a substantial amount of sunlight for healthy growth. To ensure optimal health, the plant should be protected from the midday sun's harsh rays.

Fertilization: Fertilize once every 2-3 months during the growing season with a liquid flower fertilizer mixed at half strength.

SUITABLE FOR:
Bedroom, Bathroom, Kitchen, Living Room, East or North-facing window

Goldfish Plant
Nematanthus gregarius (Family: Gesneriaceae)

☀ LIGHT	💧 WATER	🌡 TEMPARATURE	% HUMIDITY	🐾 PETS
Ideal: partial sun Tolerate: full shade	Every week	65-75°F (18-24°C)	Moderate (50-60%)	Safe for Cats and Dogs

CARING GUIDE

Water: Water generously and keep the soil continuously moist. Be aware that the soil should never dry completely out.

Light: Goldfish plant thrives in an environment that gets substantial sun exposure but not constant. Nevertheless, its tolerance to shaded conditions is remarkable.

Fertilization: Prefers biweekly fertilization during the growing season. Use a balanced slow-release or liquid diluted fertilizer.

SUITABLE FOR:
Bedroom, Bathroom, Kitchen, Living Room, Children's Room, East or North-facing window

Also known as: Candy Corn Plant, Guppy Plant

The Goldfish plant is the living aquarium for your window! This trailing cutie, reaching about 30cm tall, loves to hang out in baskets and surprise you with orange blooms all spring and summer. But it is not your typical flower – its petals morph into tiny goldfish, complete with a bit of yellow "mouth" begging for a snack. Just keep it happy with the light shade or indirect sunlight.

The Goldfish Plant (Nematanthus gregarius) is native to Brazil, particularly in the Atlantic Forest biome. The genus name "Nematanthus" is derived from the Greek words "nema," meaning "thread," and "anthos," meaning "flower." This refers to the plant's slender, thread-like stems. "Gregarius" is Latin for "gregarious" or "sociable," referring to the plant's clustered growth habit. The common name "Goldfish Plant" is inspired by the orange blooms' resemblance to goldfish. While the exact date of discovery of this plant is not well-documented, the plant was likely discovered during the period of intense botanical exploration in South America when European botanists were cataloging new species.

HEART OF JESUS
Caladium hortulanum (Family: Araceae)

LIGHT
Ideal: Partial sun
Tolerate: Full shade

WATER
Every Week

TEMPERATURE
65-80°F
(18-27°C)

HUMIDITY
High
(60-80%)

PETS
Not Safe for Cats and Dogs

Also known as: Elephant's ear, Angel wings

With leaves resembling delicate hearts, the Heart of Jesus is captivating. Native to the lush rainforests of South America, this plant has found a new home in the balmy climate around Lake Placid, Florida. There, it has blossomed into a beloved centerpiece for an annual festival, its vibrant foliage adding a touch of tropical flair to the festivities.

Caladium hortulanum, commonly known as the Heart of Jesus or Angel Wings, is steeped in fascinating tales and facts that reflect its captivating allure. The name "Heart of Jesus" is inspired by the plant's heart-shaped leaves. In many cultures, the heart symbolizes love, devotion, and spiritual connection, which may explain why this name is associated with a religious figure like Jesus. The name suggests a spiritual or divine love, possibly indicating the plant's perceived sacred or blessed nature. Myths surrounding the Heart of Jesus often revolve around its mystical powers, with legends suggesting that keeping one in the home brings harmony and understanding among family members.

CARING GUIDE

Water: Having a tuberous base, which means water and nutrients are stored in its vessel, you can water about once a week

Light: Thrives under moderate sun exposure, but also tolerates relatively low lighting conditions. Its origin environment has a conducive balance of shadow and light.

Fertilization: Feed with a good fertilizer (5-10-10 or 5-10-5 are good options) every four to six weeks during the growing season.

SUITABLE FOR:
Bedroom, Bathroom, East or North-facing window

INCH PLANT
Tradescantia zebrina (FAMILY: Commelinaceae)

LIGHT	WATER	TEMPERATURE	HUMIDITY	PETS
Ideal: Partial sun	Every Week	65-80°F (18-27°C)	High (60-80%)	Not Safe for Cats and Dogs
Tolerate: Full sun, Full shade				

CARING GUIDE

Water: It does not do well if its soil is over wet or dry. So water deeply, and allow its soil to dry between waterings

Light: Silver inch plant prefers partial sun, favoring the soft rays of morning or evening. It can adapt to significant sunlight, or manage less in shaded conditions.

Fertilization: Does not require fertilizer. If fertilization is preferred, a general-purpose commercial fertilizer should be used.

SUITABLE FOR:
Bedroom, Bathroom, Kitchen, Living Room, Office/Study Room, Balcony/Patio, East or North-facing window

Also known as: Wandering Jew, Spiderwort, Purple Heart

Inch plant, a captivating cascade of beauty, is ideal for indoor enthusiasts. Its striking foliage, a blend of green, silver, and purple, cascades gracefully from hanging pots or shelves, adding a touch of tropical elegance to any room. This easy-to-care-for charm, sometimes referred to as Wandering Jew, thrives in sunny spots, making it an ideal choice to brighten your home.

The Inch Plant, scientifically known as Tradescantia zebrina, is native to Mexico and Central America. It was introduced to Europe in the 19th century and quickly became popular as an ornamental plant. The genus name "Tradescantia" honors John Tradescant the Elder (c.1570s–1638), a notable English botanist and gardener. Tradescant was a pioneering plant collector who introduced many new species to England. while "Zebrina" is derived from the Latin word "zebrinus," meaning "like a zebra." This refers to the plant's zebra-like, striped leaves, a key feature of this species. Its common name, "The Inch Plant," refers to its fast-growing nature, where it can grow an inch or more in a week under ideal conditions.

JADE PLANT
Crassula ovata (FAMILY: Crassulaceae)

LIGHT	WATER	TEMPARATURE	HUMIDITY	PETS
Ideal: Partial sun Tolerate: Full sun, Full shade	Every 3 weeks	65-75°F (18-24°C)	Low (20-40%)	Not Safe for Cats and Dogs

Also known as: Money Plant, Lucky Plant, Friendship Tree

Resembling a miniature tree from a whimsical fairy tale, the jade plant has long captivated hearts worldwide as one of the most beloved succulents. The Jade Plant, exceptionally well-suited to contemporary indoor environments, effortlessly thrives in homes' warm, dry air. Its lifespan is remarkably long, allowing its cherished presence to be lovingly passed down through generations.

The Jade Plant, known scientifically as Crassula ovata, is a succulent plant native to Mozambique and South Africa. The genus name "Crassula" comes from the Latin word "Crassus," meaning thick or fat, referring to the thick leaves of many plants in this genus. "Ovata" is derived from Latin, meaning egg-shaped, which describes the form of its leaves. In various cultures, particularly in East Asian folklore, the Jade Plant is seen as a symbol of prosperity, luck, and good fortune. It's commonly placed in business establishments or homes, believed to bring financial success. Traditionally, the Jade Plant has been used by the Khoikhoi, and other African tribes used it to treat epilepsy and make corn beer.

CARING GUIDE

Water: Jade plant is very susceptible to root rot, so be sure its soil gets to dry out completely in between waterings.

Light: Prefers moderate light exposure, that is slightly filtered. It still endures considerable light contrasts, intense illumination to considerably diminished light.

Fertilization: Fertilize when roots are moist to avoid damage. A water-soluble, succulents fertilizer twice a year is sufficient.

SUITABLE FOR:
Bedroom, Kitchen, Living Room, Office/Study Room, Balcony/Patio, South or West-facing window

KALANCHOE

Kalanchoe blossfeldiana (FAMILY: Crassulaceae)

LIGHT	WATER	TEMPERATURE	HUMIDITY	PETS
Ideal: Partial sun Tolerate: Full sun, Full shade	Every 3 weeks	60-80°F (15-27°C)	Moderate (40-60%)	Not Safe for Cats and Dogs

CARING GUIDE

Water: As it can hold water in its leaves, water thoroughly once its soil allowed to dry out completely between waterings.

Light: Thrives under moderate sunlight exposure, not completely shaded, but not under intense full-day sun. It can also endure stages of less or more light exposure.

Fertilization: Should be fed each month with a flowering plant fertilizer. Feeding this species once is sufficient during winter.

SUITABLE FOR:
Bedroom, Kitchen, Living Room, Balcony/Patio, South or West-facing window

Also known as: Flaming Katy, Christmas Kalanchoe

Hailing from the enchanting island of Madagascar, the florist Kalanchoe, also known as Kalanchoe blossfeldiana, has graced our homes as a beloved houseplant since the 1930s. Unlike its succulent counterparts, often admired for their unique foliage, the florist kalanchoe captivates the viewer with its vibrant flowerheads that burst forth in vibrant hues during the autumn and winter.

Kalanchoe blossfeldiana is often known for its vibrant flowers and succulent qualities. The name "Kalanchoe" comes from the phonetic transcription of "Kalanchauhuy," which is derived from the Chinese name of one of the species. It's commonly called Flaming Katy, Christmas Kalanchoe, Florist Kalanchoe, and Madagascar Widow's-Thrill. These names often reflect the plant's vibrant appearance and its popularity around specific holidays like Christmas. Kalanchoe blossfeldiana was first introduced to the botanical world by Robert Blossfeld, a German botanist, in 1932. He was responsible for its cultivation and introduction into the European market, which subsequently led to its global popularity.

LIPSTICK PLANT
Aeschynanthus radicans (FAMILY: Gesneraceae)

LIGHT	WATER	TEMPARATURE	HUMIDITY	PETS
Ideal: Partial sun Tolerate: full sun	Every Week	60-75°F (15-24°C)	High (60-70%)	Safe for Cats and Dogs

Also known as: Lipstick Vine, Basket Vine

The Lipstick Plant is a tropical cutie with juicy green leaves and flowers that bloom like tiny red tubes of sunshine. Seriously, it's like lipstick kisses on your windowsill! No wonder this beauty has traveled the world – everyone wants a piece of the action. And the best part? It's low-maintenance, so you can focus on admiring its fiery blooms and not stressing about keeping it happy.

The name "Lipstick Plant" primarily stems from its distinctive shape. The vibrant red color of the flowers, combined with their shape, evokes the image of rolled-up lipstick. The Lipstick Plant's scientific name, Aeschynanthus radicans, translates to "blooming flower with roots." This elegant name hints at the plant's ability to grow and flower even when its roots have limited access to soil, making it a natural for hanging baskets and vertical gardens. In some regions, the Lipstick Plant is believed to bring good luck in love and marriage. It may be gifted to couples or planted around the home to attract love. The tubular shape of the flowers is an adaptation for pollination by hummingbirds in its native habitat.

CARING GUIDE

Water: Water deeply until pot drainage starts at the bottom of the pot. Then, wait for the soil to dry before repeating.

Light: Prefers moderate to abundant sunlight, allowing it to cultivate its vibrant foliage. Not enough light may hinder its growth and too much can scorch its leaves.

Fertilization: Fertilize every 2-3 weeks in spring and summer. High nitrogen, medium phosphorous, and low potassium.

SUITABLE FOR:
Bedroom, Bathroom, Kitchen, Living Room, Office/Study Room, East or North-facing window

LILY OF THE VALLEY
Convallaria majalis (FAMILY: Asparagaceae)

LIGHT	WATER	TEMPERATURE	HUMIDITY	PETS
Ideal: Partial sun Tolerate: Full shade	Every Week	45-65°F (7-18°C)	Moderate (40-60%)	Not Safe for Cats and Dogs

Also known as: May Lily, Our Lady's Tears, Convall Lily

Lily of the Valley has captivated hearts with its enchanting fragrance and blossoms. Despite its hidden danger, as it is a highly poisonous plant, the lily of the valley's allure has earned it a place in gardens and the perfume industry. However, it's crucial to exercise caution when bringing lily of the valley into your home, as its toxicity poses a risk to pets and children.

The name "Lily of the Valley" is somewhat misleading as the plant is not a true lily. It belongs to the genus Convallaria, while true lilies belong to the genus Lilium. The genus name Convallaria is derived from Latin, meaning "of the valley," aptly describing its natural habitat. The species name majalis or majus refers to its flowering time, which is typically in May. May 1st is known as "World Lily of the Valley Day." In France, it's a tradition to give these flowers on May

CARING GUIDE

Water: Needs consistent and adequate watering to thrive. Lily of the valley is so sensitive to drought and waterlogging.

Light: Flourishes under a mix of sun and cloud, and can thrive even in completely clouded conditions, mirroring their origin environment of dappled woodland floors.

Fertilization: Doesn't need, but for bigger blooms, add diluted fertilizer with no nitrogen, once a week in the early summer.

SUITABLE FOR:
Bathroom, East or North-facing window

Day as a symbol of springtime and good luck. Besides "Lily of the Valley," it's also known as "May Bells," "Mary's Tears," and "Our Lady's Tears" in different cultures, reflecting its blooming in May and various religious and cultural associations. Lily of the Valley was a favorite flower of Queen Victoria and has been included in numerous royal bouquets, including Kate Middleton's wedding bouquet when she married Prince William. In religious texts, it's often associated with humility and chastity, connected to the Virgin Mary in Christian iconography. Traditionally, it was used for medicinal purposes, though it is toxic if consumed. Its use ranged from cardiac treatments to epilepsy, but modern medicine has largely replaced these uses due to the plant's toxicity. The appearance of Lily of the Valley in both literature and visual media underscores its dual nature - a symbol of purity and beauty but also of hidden danger.

MONEY TREE

Pachira aquatica (FAMILY: Malvaceae)

LIGHT	WATER	TEMPARATURE	HUMIDITY	PETS
Ideal: Partial sun	Every	60-70°F	Moderate	Safe for Cats
Tolerate: full sun	2 weeks	(15-21°C)	(40-50%)	and Dogs

CARING GUIDE

Water: Keep the soil moist, checking it every few days for dryness. Watering will vary upon the weather and air humidity.

Light: Needs a lot of indirect or filtered light when grown indoors, a good rule of thumb is a minimum of 6 hours, including up to 3-6 hours of direct sunlight per day.

Fertilization: Apply a water-soluble balanced fertilizer 3-4 times during the growing season. Or apply a slow-release formula.

SUITABLE FOR:

Bedroom, Bathroom, Kitchen, Living Room, Office/Study Room, Children's Room, East or North-facing window

Also known as: Guiana Chestnut, Malabar Chestnut

This cheerful houseplant hails from tropical swamps, where it drinks in sunshine and warmth. Though its name comes from a whimsical legend, many believe it brings good luck. In fact, some even braid its trunks like tiny tree-ventails, making it a real charmer. Just a heads-up, science whispers its nuts might not be the friendliest, so best keep those for admiring, not munching.

The Money Tree has roots in East Asian cultures. Legend has it that a poor farmer prayed for wealth, found the plant in the wild, and cultivated it. As the plant brought him prosperity, it became a symbol of good fortune. The five-lobed leaves of the Money Tree are often associated with the five elements in traditional Chinese philosophy: wood, water, fire, metal, and earth. The balance of these elements is believed to bring harmony and prosperity. Some legends state that a poor man braided the trunks of several Pachira aquatica plants together, and as a result, his financial situation improved. The practice of braiding the trunks is thought to enhance the plant's power to attract wealth.

MOTH ORCHID
Phalaenopsis (Family: Orchidaceae)

LIGHT	WATER	TEMPARATURE	HUMIDITY	PETS
Ideal: Partial sun / Tolerate: full shade	Every Week	60-75°F (15-24°C)	Moderate (50-60%)	Safe for Cats and Dogs

Also known as: Moon Orchid, Phal, mariposa orchid

The moth orchid is a vision of elegance with its delicate blooms. This houseplant charmer thrives with just a bit of love. Like graceful ballerinas, its cascading flowers can stay on show for months! Just keep its roots company with regular sips of water and find a spot bathed in gentle, indirect sunlight. This easygoing beauty will reward you with months of blooming bliss.

The Moth Orchid (Phalaenopsis) is native to Southeast Asia, the Philippines, and Australia. They were discovered in the late 17th century by European explorers but gained popularity in the 19th century when Victorian-era fascination with orchids peaked. In the 19th century, the cultivation of orchids, including Phalaenopsis, became so popular in Europe that it was termed "Orchidelirium." Wealthy enthusiasts sent collectors around the world to find new species. It is named "Phalaenopsis" for its resemblance to moths, derived from the Greek words "phalaina," meaning "moth," and "opsis," meaning "resembling". This resemblance is most noticeable when the flowers are in full bloom and viewed from a distance.

CARING GUIDE

Water: Water weekly or when aerial roots turn silvery, cutting back in damp weather and increasing when it is hot or dry.

Light: Prefers a moderate sun, but it can also survive in a shade with less light. This light adaptability is a characteristic retained from its original environment.

Fertilization: Feed with half-strength orchid fertilizer every 2-3 weeks during the growing season. Don't fertilize while blooming

SUITABLE FOR:
Bedroom, Bathroom, Kitchen, Living Room, Office/Study Room, Children's Room, East or North-facing window

MONSTERA
Monstera deliciosa (FAMILY: Araceae)

LIGHT	WATER	TEMPERATURE	HUMIDITY	PETS
Ideal: Partial sun Tolerate: Full shade	Every Week	60-80°F (15-27°C)	Moderate (40-60%)	Not Safe for Cats and Dogs

Also known as: Swiss Cheese Plant, Fruit Salad Plant

From the lush rainforests of Central America, the monstera deliciosa has escaped into our homes as a captivating houseplant. Like polished emeralds, its leaves boast a curious secret: tiny holes that whisper tales of jungle adventures. But fear not; this Swiss cheese plant is all charm. When ripe, its long, corncob-like fruit bursts with a sweet, intoxicating perfume.

The Monstera deliciosa, commonly known as the Swiss cheese plant, is native to regions from southern Mexico to Panama. The specific epithet "deliciosa" translates to "delicious," referring to the edible fruit the plant produces. The genus name "Monstera" is derived from the Latin word for "monstrous," which relates to the plants' unusual leaves that often have natural holes. Common names for the Monstera deliciosa include delicious monster, fruit salad plant, and several

CARING GUIDE

Water: Avoid overwatering as it is susceptible to root rot. Watered it after the top few inches of potting soil dry out.

Fertilization: Provide a balanced fertilizer. Diluted liquid fertilizer every 2-3 months will work for fertilizing this species.

Light: Prefers a moderate amount of light, and can tolerate lower light conditions. Originating from where it grew under the dappled glow of larger plants.

SUITABLE FOR:
Bedroom, Bathroom, Kitchen, Living Room, Office/Study Room, South or West-facing window

others, each reflecting different cultural associations of the plant. Historically, Monstera deliciosa has been used for various purposes. In Peru, the aerial roots of the plant were used as ropes, and in Mexico, they were crafted into baskets. The root of the plant has also been utilized in Martinique as a remedy for snakebites. French botanist Charles Plumier was the first to mention the Monstera plant in Western literature, dating back to 1693. who described the plant's leaf structure, inflorescence, root dimorphism, and its use in treating snake bites. However, he did not know the name at the time. The plant was introduced to Europe around 1832 when Wilhelm Friederich von Karwinsky collected a herbarium specimen from Mexico. Josef Ritter von Warszewicz later cultivated it in the Berlin Botanic Gardens in 1849, and by 1858, the plant was bearing fruit in the Royal Botanic Gardens in Kew, United Kingdom.

Norfolk Island Pine
Araucaria heterophylla (Family: Araucariaceae)

Light	Water	Temparature	Humidity	Pets
Ideal: Partial sun Tolerate: Full sun, Full shade	Every 1-2 weeks	50-70°F (10-21°C)	Moderate (50-60%)	Not Safe for Cats and Dogs

CARING GUIDE

Water: Water your norfolk island pine as frequently as needed to maintain damp soil, usually once every couple of weeks.

Light: Favors conditions where it can get a fair share of sun throughout the day, while being capable of withstanding considerable shade or well-lit environments alike.

Fertilization: Fertilize every 2-4 weeks during the growing season. Use a liquid plant food for your indoor norfolk island pine.

SUITABLE FOR: Living Room, Children's Room, East or North-facing window

Also known as: Star Pine, Star Christmas Tree, House Pine

With their rich green and delicate evergreen needles, Norfolk Island pines make beautiful additions to houseplant collections, particularly around the holiday season. They offer a delightful alternative for decorating, serving as a smaller version of the traditional family Christmas tree! Although popular during the festive period, they are also readily available year-round.

The name "Norfolk Island Pine" refers to the tree's native habitat, Norfolk Island. Europeans first discovered the tree when Captain James Cook arrived at Norfolk Island in 1774. This genus name "Araucaria" is derived from the Arauco Indians of central Chile, where the first species of Araucaria was discovered. This specific epithet, "heterophylla," comes from the Greek words "heteros" (meaning different) and "phyllon" (meaning leaf), referring to the variation in the plant's leaves throughout its life. Although it's not a true pine, the Norfolk Island Pine is often used as a living Christmas tree in warmer climates due to its conical shape. This tradition has made it a popular holiday plant in many households.

OCTOPUS PLANT
Tillandsia Caput Medusae (Family: Bromeliaceae)

LIGHT	WATER	TEMPERATURE	HUMIDITY	PETS
Ideal: Partial sun Tolerate: full sun	Every Day	50-75°F (10-24°C)	Moderate (30-50%)	Safe for Cats and Dogs

Also known as: Medusa Air Plant, Medusa's head

One of the most well-liked members of the Tillandsia genus is a flowering air plant from the Bromeliads family. This plant is known as Caput Medusae and has an unusual appearance and growth pattern that sets it apart from other indoor plants. As long as you pay attention to its unorthodox needs and provide proper care, this tillandsia does not even challenge an inexpert hand.

The Octopus plant is aptly named for its swirling tendril-like leaves reminiscent of a sea creature's arms. It was named by the Swedish botanist Carl Linnaeus, who is often referred to as the "father of modern taxonomy." Its scientific name, Tillandsia Caput Medusae, pays homage to the mythical Gorgon, Medusa, whose hair was said to be a writhing mass of snakes. This connection is further emphasized by the plant's alternate name, Medusa's Head, highlighting its captivating, Medusa-esque beauty. But beyond its striking appearance, the Octopus plant carries no sinister curse. Instead, it thrives, drawing sustenance from the air and rain, much like a mythical creature unbound by earthly constraints.

CARING GUIDE

Water: It does not prefer much water. Minimal watering is advised, keep the soil moist but do not let water accumulate.

Light: Prefers well-lit environment with sufficient, not excessive, exposure to rays of the sun. Too much sunlight can, however, lead to harmful effects like leaf burn.

Fertilization: Fertilize it mixing in a balanced diluted liquid fertilizer with the water once a month during the growing season.

SUITABLE FOR:
Bedroom, Bathroom, Kitchen, Living Room, Office/Study Room, Balcony/Patio, East or North-facing window

PINK PRINCESS

Philodendron erubescens (FAMILY: Araceae)

LIGHT	WATER	TEMPERATURE	HUMIDITY	PETS
Ideal: partial sun Tolerate: full shade	Every Week	65-75°F (18-24°C)	Moderate (50-60%)	Not Safe for Cats and Dogs

CARING GUIDE

Water: Allow the soil to dry between deep waterings. Ensure it is never sitting in waterlogged soil to prevent root rot.

Light: Pink princess prefers a location that receives several hours of bright, indirect light. When grown indoors, it can also tolerate a couple hours of direct light.

Fertilization: During spring and summer, pink princess benefits from regular monthly feedings with a balanced liquid fertilizer.

SUITABLE FOR:
Bedroom, Bathroom, Kitchen, Office/Study Room, East or North-facing window

Also known as: Blushing philodendron

The Pink Princess Philodendron is a highly sought-after plant due to its unique and stable variegation. Its deep green, heart-shaped leaves are adorned with bubblegum pink markings, making it a standout in any collection. Unlike the similar Philodendron Pink Congo, whose variegation is chemically induced and fades over time, the Pink Princess's variegation is natural and long-lasting.

The Pink Princess Philodendron, a native of Colombia and Ecuador, was first described in 1870. It's believed to have been discovered by an Austrian botanist named Heinrich Schott. However, it wasn't until the 1970s that the variegated form, now known as the Pink Princess, was discovered in a Florida greenhouse. The name "Philodendron erubescens" is a blend of Greek and Latin words, revealing the plant's intriguing nature. "Philodendron," derived from "phileo" (love) and "dendron" (tree), embracing trees for support. "Erubescens," rooted in the Latin "erubescere" (to blush), captures the blushing red hue of its stems and leaf undersides. Together, they paint a picture of a blushing tree-lover with undeniable charm.

PAINTED NETTLE
Plectranthus scutellarioides (Family: Lamiaceae)

☀️ LIGHT	💧 WATER	🌡️ TEMPARATURE	💧 HUMIDITY	🧪 PETS
Ideal: Partial sun Tolerate: full sun	Every Week	65-75°F (18-24°C)	Moderate (50-60%)	Not Safe for Cats and Dogs

Also known as: Indian Borage, Coleus, Spanish Thyme

Adding a pop of color to your surroundings has never been easier with the charming Painted Nettle. The painted nettle stands out with its vivid foliage, captivating the eye. Its leaves display a stunning spectrum of colors, ranging from yellow and red to purple, making the plant a true work of art. Cultivate it and relish the beauty it brings, enhancing your garden's aesthetic appeal!

Painted Nettle, scientifically known as Plectranthus scutellarioides, is celebrated for its colorful foliage. The name "Plectranthus" derives from the Greek "plectron" (spur) and "anthos" (flower), reflecting the spur-shaped flowers in this genus. Its species name, "scutellarioides," originates from "scutellaria" and "-oides" (meaning resembling), indicating the similarity to Scutellaria species' flowers. The Painted Nettle's leaves change color based on sunlight exposure; more sunlight leads to brighter leaf colors. It was once part of the Coleus genus, and many people still know it by its old name, Coleus. This frequent reclassification in botany showcases the evolving nature of plant taxonomy.

CARING GUIDE

Water: Frequent watering and maintaining high local humidity can result in an optimally flourishing Painted Nettle.

Light: Flourishes best with a fair amount of sun daily, though it can withstand exposure to intense sunlight. However, inadequate sun can lead to weak growth.

Fertilization: Fertilize during the summer growing season with an all-purpose fertilizer (high-nitrogen is recommended).

SUITABLE FOR: Kitchen, Living Room, Office/Study Room, West or South-facing window

Ponytail Palm

Beaucarnea recurvata (Family: Asparagaceae)

Light	Water	Temparature	Humidity	Pets
Ideal: Full sun Tolerate: Partial sun	Every 3 weeks	50-70°F (10-21°C)	Moderate (40-50%)	Safe for Cats and Dogs

CARING GUIDE

Water: Water an average of every two weeks. The frequency will vary from weekly in summer to maybe once a month in winter.

Light: Ponytail palm is typically acclimated to areas where it's regularly exposed to moderate sunlight, with the ability to tolerate complete, sun and shade exposure.

Fertilization: Use a quarter dose of liquid fertilizer, high potassium and low nitrogen once a month during spring and summer.

SUITABLE FOR:
Bedroom, Kitchen, Living Room, Balcony/Patio, Children's Room, South or West-facing window

Also known as: Elephant's Foot, Bottle Palm

The captivating ponytail palm is a popular houseplant featuring a cascade of leaves that resemble a ponytail. Adaptable and resilient, this plant is a favorite for its unique appearance and low-maintenance needs. Known for their ease of care and forgiving nature, just give it bright light and the occasional sip of water, and let your ponytail palm be the life of your leafy party.

Originating from arid regions of Mexico, the Ponytail Palm (Beaucarnea recurvata) is a resilient plant with a trunk that swells at the base, earning it the common name "elephant's foot." Despite its name, the Ponytail Palm is not a true palm but a member of the Agave family. Its long, cascading leaves give it a distinctive ponytail-like appearance. The name "Beaucarnea" pays homage to Jean-Baptiste Beaucarne, a 19th-century Belgian horticulturist. The species name "recurvata" refers to the curving back, or recurved nature, of the plant's leaves. Traditionally, the plant was valued for its water storage capabilities. The swollen base of the trunk stores water, making it highly resilient in arid environments.

SAGO PALM
Cycas revoluta (FAMILY: Cycadaceae)

LIGHT	WATER	TEMPERATURE	HUMIDITY	PETS
Ideal: Partial sun Tolerate: Full sun, Full shade	Every 1-2 weeks	60-75°F (15-24°C)	Moderate (40-60%)	Not Safe for Cats and Dogs

Also known as: King Sago, Japanese Sago Palm, Sago Palm

Sago palms are indoor houseplants with a slow growth rate, taking several years to reach their maximum height of 2ft. These plants typically produce only one leaf per year. The sago palm is the only cycas plant from its genus available for purchase in garden stores as an indoor houseplant. Its fronds and overall structure lend a tropical ambiance and a natural, exotic touch to any room.

The Sago Palm (Cycas revoluta) is not a true palm (family Arecaceae) but belongs to the Cycad family (Cycadaceae). The genus name "Cycas" is derived from the Greek word "kykas," which is believed to be a transcription error of the word "koikas," meaning "palm tree." This reflects the superficial resemblance of cycads like the Sago Palm to true palms. The species name "revoluta" comes from Latin, meaning "rolled back," referring to the characteristic curled leaves. Cycas revoluta, native to Japan, has been known for centuries. The most notable use of Cycas revoluta is the extraction of sago from the trunk. This starch has been a traditional food source in some cultures, especially Japan and the Ryukyu Islands.

CARING GUIDE

Water: It should be watered both regularly and consistently. It should be allowed to dry out prior to being watered again.

Light: Prefers to be in moderate sunlight and can tolerate both heavy shade conditions and intense sunlight. It can healthily thrive across a range of light levels.

Fertilization: Does well with fertilizing in its growing season. Palm fertilizer of 12-4-12 should be given from spring to fall.

SUITABLE FOR:
Balcony/Patio, South or West-facing window

Scarlet Star

Guzmania lingulata (Family: Bromeliaceae)

☀ Light	💧 Water	🌡 Temperature	💧 Humidity	🐾 Pets
Ideal: Partial sun Tolerate: Full shade	Every Week	65-75°F (18-24°C)	High (60-70%)	Safe for Cats and Dogs

Also known as: Scarlet Star Bromeliad, Blushing Bromeliad

The Scarlet star (Guzmania lingulata) is a tropical charmer who loves hanging out indoors and boasting vibrant red or orange blooms that can last for months. Originally from the rainforests of South and Central America, it adapted perfectly to living the houseplant life. Just give a bright spot and a little water in a cup-shaped center, and you will be rewarded with exotic flair all year round.

Scarlet Star (Guzmania lingulata) is native to the rainforests of Central and South America. Its botanical identity, "Guzmania," refers to the Spanish naturalist Anastasio Guzman, who made significant contributions to the study of these plants, and the Latin word "lingulata," meaning tongue-shaped, refers to the shape of the plant's leaves. "Scarlet Star" is named for its scarlet star-like bracts surrounding the small, inconspicuous flowers. In contemporary culture, it symbolizes exotic beauty and is often used in tropical-themed decor. The Scarlet Star belongs to the Bromeliaceae family, which also includes pineapples. This family is known for its unique adaptations to diverse environments.

CARING GUIDE

Water: Water weekly or whenever the top inch of soil dries out. Water deeply but make sure to avoid water accumulation.

Light: Scarlet-star prefers a balance between ample light and shade. Too much light can cause leaf scorching while little light can lead to lackluster foliage growth.

Fertilization: During spring and summer, fertilize once every 2 months with a balanced water-soluble fertilizer at half strength.

SUITABLE FOR:

Bedroom, Bathroom, Kitchen, Living Room, Balcony/Patio, Children's Room, East or North-facing window

STAR JASMINE
Trachelospermum jasminoides (Family: Apocynaceae)

☀ LIGHT	💧 WATER	🌡 TEMPARATURE	💧 HUMIDITY	🐾 PETS
Ideal: Full sun Tolerate: Partial sun	Every Week	50-70°F (10-21°C)	Moderate (50-60%)	Safe for Cats and Dogs

Also known as: Confederate Jasmine, Chinese Star Jasmine

This charmer, Star Jasmine, is a fragrant friend and a total globe-trotter! Sun or shade doesn't fuss; it just fills your home with its sweet perfume and easygoing vibes. It's a natural climber, happiest scaling walls or fences, where it unfurls its star-shaped blooms and attracts a buzzing crowd of bee buddies. Even if you're a busy plant parent, this jasmine's the perfect companion.

The Star Jasmine is not a true member of the Jasmine family. Instead, it belongs to the Apocynaceae family. Its scientific name, Trachelospermum jasminoidese, is Derived from Greek, "Trachelospermum" refers to the elongated seed pods found along its stem, while "jasminoides" signifies its resemblance to jasmine. Interestingly, its common name, Confederate jasmine, holds two possible origins. One theory suggests Confederate soldiers brought it to the Southern United States from Mexico. Alternatively, it might have been named after the Malay Confederacy, a former British colony in Southeast Asia where early explorers likely encountered the plant and associated its fragrant white flowers with the jasmine.

> **CARING GUIDE**
>
> **Water:** Star jasmine requires plenty of water during the growing season, but it is rarely thirsty during fall and winter.
>
> **Light:** Prefers a mix of sun and shade. Tolerating full sun or full shade, but too much sunlight causes leaf scorch, and prolonged shade can result in sparse flowering.
>
> **Fertilization:** Mulching the soil at the start of the season provides added nutrients. Use a slow-release fertilizer once a year.
>
> **SUITABLE FOR:** Living Room, Balcony/Patio, South or West-facing window

Ti Plant
Cordyline fruticosa (FAMILY: Asparagaceae)

☀️ LIGHT	💧 WATER	🌡️ TEMPERATURE	💧 HUMIDITY	🧪 PETS
Ideal: Partial sun Tolerate: Full sun, Full shade	Every 1-2 weeks	60-80°F (15-27°C)	Moderate (40-60%)	Not Safe for Cats and Dogs

Also known as: Palm Lily, Cabbage palm

The Ti plant is a cultural symbol and also super helpful. Tall and proud like a palm, it whispers ancient stories in some Austronesian cultures, bridging the gap between the living and those who have passed. But it's not just a spiritual sage; this beauty is a crafty chameleon! Its leaves turn into awesome dyes, making fabrics super colorful! It's like painting with island sunshine vibes.

Ti Plant, scientifically known as Cordyline fruticosa, is a tropical perennial plant with a rich history and a variety of uses. The common name "Ti Plant" is derived from its Pacific Islands origins, where it is pronounced as "tee." This name is prevalent in Hawaii and across Polynesia. Cordyline" derives from the Greek word 'kordyle,' meaning "club," a reference to the plant's club-like roots. "Fruticosa" is Latin, meaning "shrubby" or "bushy," referring to the plant's growth habit.

CARING GUIDE

Water: Water Ti plant only when the top few inches of soil dry out. Use distilled water, and avoid wetting the leaves.

Light: Flourishes under moderate sunlight, and able to tolerate wide range of light exposure, from ample sun to scarce light, and can also endure lower light levels.

Fertilization: Use a slow-release, balanced fertilizer. During the growing season, you can use a liquid fertilizer once a month.

SUITABLE FOR:
Living Room, Balcony/Patio, East or North-facing window

Besides "Ti Plant," it is also known as "Cabbage Palm" and "Good Luck Plant," reflecting its appearance and the beliefs associated with it. In Polynesian culture, the Ti Plant is considered sacred to the gods, particularly to Lono, the god of fertility and music, and Laka, the goddess of hula dance. This association makes the plant a key element in religious ceremonies and rituals. The Ti Plant is frequently mentioned in traditional Hawaiian chants and hulas, where it symbolizes various themes, from love to divine power. The Ti Plant is believed to have strong protective properties. In ancient Hawaii, it was thought to ward off evil spirits. Planting a Ti Plant around homes was a common practice for spiritual protection and purification. The leaves of the Ti Plant are so strong and durable that early Polynesians used them as makeshift survival tools, including for wrapping and cooking food, and even as makeshift plates.

Umbrella Tree

Schefflera arboricola (Family: Araliaceae)

Light	Water	Temperature	Humidity	Pets
Ideal: Partial sun Tolerate: Full sun, Full shade	Every 1-2 weeks	65-75°F (18-24°C)	Moderate (40-60%)	Not Safe for Cats and Dogs

CARING GUIDE

Water: Overwatering is the biggest threat. Watered regularly, and allow the soil to partially dry out between watering.

Light: Prefers moderate daily sunlight amounts and can handle a fully lit or shaded environment. Light deficiency can stunt growth, while overexposure might dry it out.

Fertilization: Use a well-balanced 10-10-10 liquid fertilizer for foliage plants, once every three weeks during spring and fall.

SUITABLE FOR:

Bedroom, Bathroom, Kitchen, Living Room, Balcony/Patio, Children's Room, East or North-facing window

Also known as: Dwarf umbrella Tree, Dwarf Schefflera

The umbrella tree, having adapted from its wild origins, has now found a cozy spot in our homes. This multi-stemmed wonder, known for its graceful leaves, thrives as a houseplant or, in warmer climates, graces gardens with its tropical elegance. But beware, its beauty comes with a hidden nibble-no: the leaves contain calcium oxalates, not ideal for pets or little fingers.

The Umbrella Tree, scientifically known as Schefflera arboricola, is native to Taiwan and Hainan, and it was introduced to other parts of the world as a decorative plant. The genus name "Schefflera" honors the German botanist Jacob Christoph Scheffler, who lived in the 18th century, reflecting the tradition of honoring scientists in the nomenclature. The specific epithet "arboricola" is Latin. It translates to "tree-dwelling," so "Schefflera arboricola" essentially means "Schefflera that is tree-dwelling" or "tree-dwelling Schefflera" The common name "Umbrella Tree" comes from the unique structure of its leaves, which are arranged in a circular pattern around a central stalk, resembling the spokes of an umbrella.

URN PLANT
Aechmea fasciata (Family: Bromeliaceae)

☀️ LIGHT	💧 WATER	🌡️ TEMPARATURE	💧 HUMIDITY	🐾 PETS
Ideal: partial sun Tolerate: full shade	Every Week	65-75°F (18-24°C)	High (60-70%)	Safe for Cats and Dogs

Also known as: Silver vase plant

The Urn plant, a silver-toned beauty, might not be the easiest housemate. It craves shade and well-draining soil, like a secret garden hidden under a canopy. And while it won't actively invite bugs to tea parties, its leafy pockets sometimes become tempting little pools for thirsty wanderers. So, if you're looking for a low-maintenance charmer, this exotic wonder might not be your best bet.

The Urn Plant, scientifically known as Aechmea fasciata, is a species of flowering plant in the bromeliad family, native to Brazil. The genus name "Aechmea" comes from the Greek word "aichme," meaning a spear. This name refers to the pointed bracts or leaves of plants in this genus. The common name "Urn Plant" is derived from the rosette shape of the plant, which resembles an urn or a vase. In the wild, Aechmea fasciata engages in a remarkable symbiotic relationship with ants, known as myrmecophily. The plant provides the ants with a secure and comfortable home within its cup-shaped structure. In return, the ants act as vigilant protectors, warding off herbivores and other pests that threaten the plant.

CARING GUIDE

Water: Prefers moisture, but not a soggy soil. Make sure the top inch of the soil is dry to the touch before you water it.

Light: Urn plant can thrive in areas that offer a mix of shade and sun, and it's able to withstand wholly shaded areas as well. It doesn't need intense sun exposure.

Fertilization: Fertilize it only from spring-to-fall. it should be given a liquid balanced fertilizer diluted to half-strength.

SUITABLE FOR:

Bedroom, Bathroom, Kitchen, Balcony/Patio, Children's Room, East or North-facing window

WAX BEGONIA

Begonia cucullata (FAMILY: Begoniaceae)

LIGHT	WATER	TEMPARATURE	HUMIDITY	PETS
Ideal: Partial sun Tolerate: Full sun, Full shade	Every Week	60-80°F (15-27°C)	Moderate (40-60%)	Not Safe for Cats and Dogs

CARING GUIDE

Water: Water regularly when the top 5 cm of soil are dry. Dont allow its roots to sit in stagnant water to avoid root rot.

Light: Prefers moderate sunlight, and tolerates sun-soaked or shaded conditions. Overexposure can damage its foliage, while insufficient light hinder growth.

Fertilization: Should be fertilized with a balanced 10-10-10 fertilizer monthly or every three weeks during the growing season.

SUITABLE FOR:

Bedroom, Bathroom, Kitchen, Living Room, Office/Study Room, Balcony/Patio, East or North-facing window

Also known as: Wax flower begonia, Clubed begonia

Originating from the vibrant landscapes of South America, wax begonia is a versatile plant that thrives in gardens and containers. Its cheerful blossoms, ranging from fiery red to delicate white and pink, add a touch of color and charm to any setting. However, wax begonia's tendency to spread enthusiastically under favorable conditions has earned it the status of an invasive species.

Wax Begonia is scientifically known as Begonia cucullata. The genus name "Begonia" honors Michel Bégon, a 17th-century French patron of botany. The species name "cucullata" is derived from Latin, meaning "hooded," which likely refers to the shape of the plant's flowers or leaves. Wax Begonias were discovered and introduced to Europe in the 17th century. They are native to South America, particularly Brazil. The plant gained popularity in Europe due to its attractive foliage and blossoms, leading to extensive cultivation. The leaves of Wax Begonias are asymmetrical, a feature known as "bilateral asymmetry." This means each leaf is divided into two unequal halves, a unique characteristic in the plant world.

YUCCA
Yucca gigantea (Family: Asparagaceae)

LIGHT	**WATER**	**TEMPARATURE**	**HUMIDITY**	**PETS**
Ideal: Partial sun Tolerate: Full sun, Full shade	Every 2-3 weeks	65-80°F (18-27°C)	Moderate (40-50%)	Not Safe for Cats and Dogs

Also known as: spineless yucca, Itabo, Yucca cane

Introducing the Yucca gigantea, a sun-seeking treasure that transforms indoor spaces with its beachy ambiance. This plant is not just about looks; it thrives with the right amount of water. A little goes a long way – water it just enough, but be careful not to overdo it. This way, your Yucca gigantea stays vibrant and lively, brightening your home with its tropical allure.

Yucca gigantea, commonly known as Yucca, is native to Central America. "Yucca" comes from the Taino word for cassava, a root vegetable unrelated to Yucca plants. The misnomer likely occurred due to early European explorers' misunderstanding of native plants in the Americas. The "gigantea" in its scientific name comes from Latin, meaning "giant"; this reflects the plant's impressive size compared to other members of the Yucca genus. Historically significant, the blossoms of Yucca gigantea are known to be edible and are used in culinary traditions. Moreover, the strong, flexible fibers from Yucca leaves were used by indigenous peoples to make durable items like ropes, baskets, and sandals.

CARING GUIDE

Water: Water every few weeks on the growing season between spring and summer, and less frequently in the fall and winter.

Light: Hailing from habitats where sun exposure varies, appreciates intermediate illumination but shows adaptability towards an abundance or minimal light.

Fertilization: Fertilize with a diluted cactus fertilizer every 2-3 months. A fertilizer with a 19-6-12 balance is recommended.

SUITABLE FOR: Living Room, Balcony/Patio, South or West-facing window

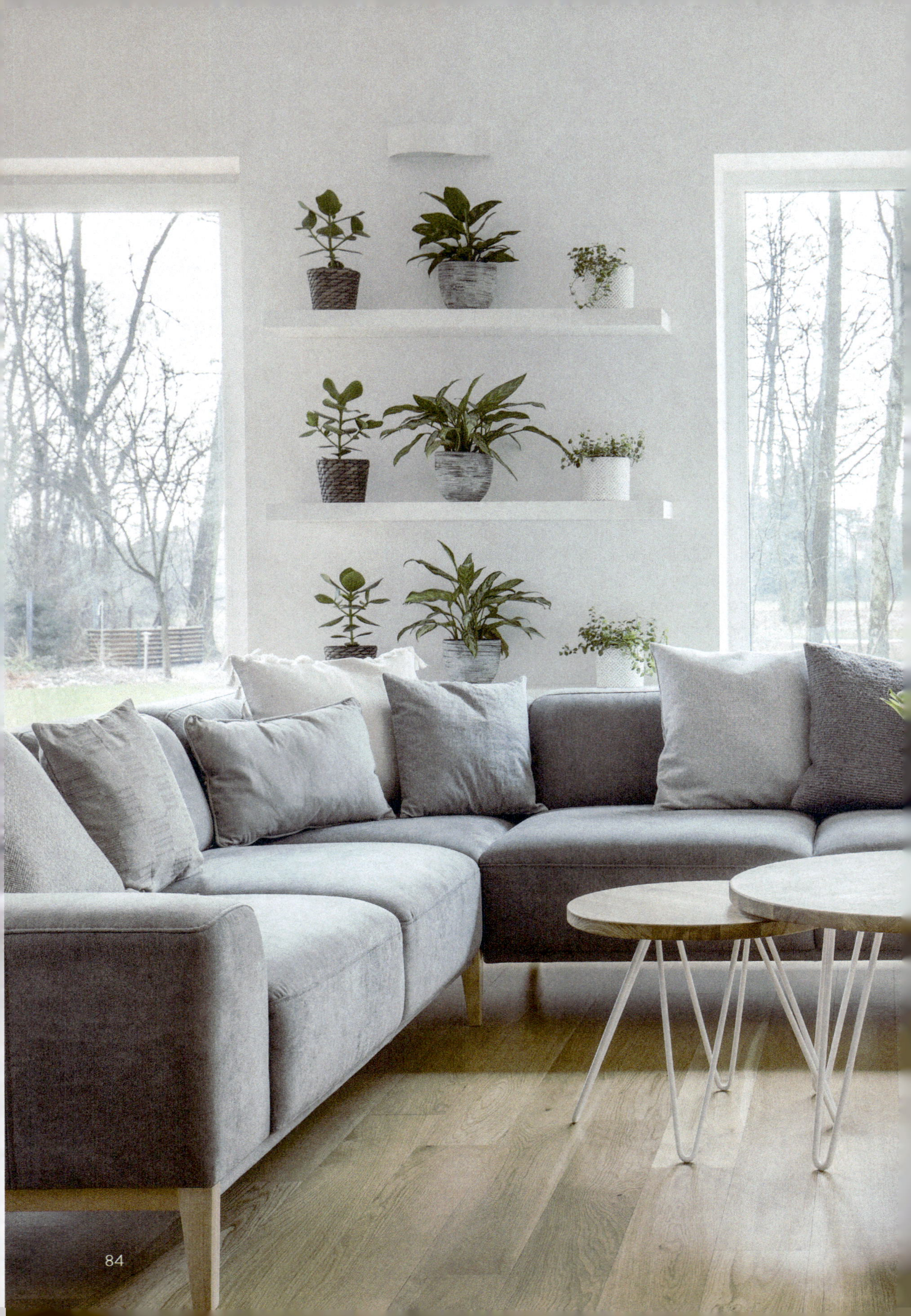

Section 3:
MEDIUM TO HIGH LIGHT PLANTS

Sunlight Lovers: Embracing Medium to High Light Plants

This section introduces Medium to High Light Plants, which flourish in abundant light, ranging from warm, filtered morning sun to intense afternoon rays. It provides essential tips on selecting the right spot for optimal light exposure, proper watering techniques, and maintaining the right temperature to keep these plants healthy. Ideal for brightening up spaces, these plants add cheerfulness to your home.

Air Plant
Tillandsia (Family: Bromeliaceae)

☀️ LIGHT	💧 WATER	🌡️ TEMPERATURE	💧 HUMIDITY	🐾 PETS
Ideal: Partial sun Tolerate: full sun	Every Week	50-75°F (10-24°C)	Moderate (30-50%)	Safe for Cats and Dogs

CARING GUIDE

Water: Soak your air plants in water for 20 minutes to an hour every week to 10 days is best. Submerge the entire plant

Light: Air plant thrives in an environment with moderate sunlight exposure, such as a mix of shade and sun, without being intensely exposed to solar radiation all day.

Fertilization: A low-maintenance plant that gets most of its nutrients from the air which means it does not need to be fertilized.

SUITABLE FOR:
Bedroom, Bathroom, Kitchen, Living Room, Office/Study Room, Balcony/Patio, East or North-facing window

Also known as: Air Plant, Sky Plant, Tillandsia

This little adventurer hails from sunny Central America, Mexico, Costa Rica, and South America, but it's become quite the Florida snowbird. Why all the love? This air plant is the ultimate low-maintenance buddy. Think of it as a tiny Tarzan, swinging freely from its perch, soaking up the good vibes and gracing your space with its spiky green charm and cheerful pops of pink blooms.

The scientific name of Air Plants, Tillandsia, was named after the Swedish physician and botanist Elias Tillandz. The Air Plant earned its common name due to its unique characteristic of acquiring nutrients and moisture from the air rather than soil. These epiphytic plants have specialized trichomes, tiny hair-like structures on their leaves, that enable them to absorb water and nutrients from the atmosphere. Tillandsia is a genus of around 650 species of evergreen, perennial flowering plants in the family Bromeliaceae, native to the forests, mountains, and deserts of the Neotropics, from northern Mexico and the southeastern United States to Mesoamerica and the Caribbean to central Argentina.

BIRD OF PARADISE
Strelitzia reginae (Family: Strelitziaceae)

LIGHT	WATER	TEMPARATURE	HUMIDITY	PETS
Ideal: Full sun Tolerate: Partial sun	Every Week	65-75°F (18-24°C)	High (60-80%)	Not Safe for Cats and Dogs

Also known as: Mini craneflower, Queen's bird-of-paradise

With its vibrant blooms resembling exotic birds in flight, the Bird of Paradise is a captivating symbol of South Africa's rich heritage. This native beauty featured on the country's 50-cent coin has also been embraced as the official flower of Los Angeles, even though it is not native. In their natural habitat, these flowers captivate sunbirds with their mesmerizing dance of color and nectar.

The Bird of Paradise (Strelitzia reginae) is a tropical flower that originates from South Africa. It is also known as the Crane Flower and has been grown at the Royal Botanic Gardens in Kew since 1773. The scientific name is Strelitzia reginae, which was named by Sir Joseph Banks, who was the director of the Royal Gardens. He named the genus Strelitzia after Queen Charlotte, the Duchess of Mecklenburg-Strelitz. The plant's flowers are unique in appearance, resembling a bird's head and beak, hence the name "Bird of Paradise.". There are other species of Strelitzia, such as Strelitzia nicolai, commonly known as the White Bird of Paradise, which is similar in appearance but larger in size.

CARING GUIDE

Water: The soil should be moist but well-drained throughout the year. It requires regular watering in warm/dry months.

Light: Thrives with abundant exposure to the sun, though it can adjust to moderate sunlight conditions. Too little light can lead to weak growth and lack of flowering.

Fertilization: Feed with a slow-release fertilizer in early spring, and with a weekly liquid fertilizer during the growing season.

SUITABLE FOR: Living Room, Balcony/Patio, Children's Room, South or West-facing window

BASIL
Ocimum basilicum (FAMILY: Lamiacea)

LIGHT	WATER	TEMPARATURE	HUMIDITY	PETS
Ideal: Full sun Tolerate: Partial sun	Twice per week	65-75°F (18-24°C)	Moderate (50-60%)	Safe for Cats and Dogs

Also known as: Saint Joseph's Wort, Common Basil

Are you craving fresh flavors and sunshine? Meet basil, your new kitchen cutie! This Asian-African mint sweetheart isn't just a pretty face - it loves regular sun and water and thrives even when you switch up its soil. Plus, those tasty, yummy leaves are packed with flavor, ready to jump from your windowsill straight onto your pizza, salads, soups, teas, and anything else you can imagine!

The name "basil" comes from the Greek word "basilikón phutón", meaning "royal/kingly plant." This could be due to the ancient tradition that only the king could harvest basil with a golden sickle. The genus name "Ocimum" is derived from the Greek word "ozo," which means "to smell," reflecting the herb's strong aroma. "Basilicum" in Latin means "royal" or "kingly," aligning with the etymology of "basil." In ancient Greece, basil was connected to the myth of the Empress

CARING GUIDE

Water: Requires its soil to be kept moist at all times. Needs frequent watering and to be kept in a well-draining pot.

Light: Prefers significant sun exposure but also endures shaded zones. Both overexposure to sunlight or a lack of it can impact plant health and growth.

Fertilization: does not need large amounts, a well-balanced fertilizer can be applied once every 4-6 weeks for indoor plants.

SUITABLE FOR:
Kitchen, Living Room, Office/Study Room, Balcony/Patio, Children's Room, South or West-facing window

of Byzantium. According to the legend, when she was looking for a suitable place to build a church dedicated to the Holy Apostles, Basil sprang up on the spot she eventually chose. This story likely contributed to basil's name, which means "kingly" or "royal" in Greek, suggesting its revered status in ancient times. In India, basil, particularly the Holy Basil (Tulsi), holds a special place in Hindu mythology. It's considered sacred to the gods Vishnu and Krishna. Tulsi is revered as a goddess in her own right and is a symbol of purity and devotion. According to a legend, Tulsi was a devoted wife who was turned into a plant by her husband as a test of her faith. Hindus often grow tulsi in their homes and temples, and it's used in daily worship. Culinary legends often attribute basil with love and passion. In Italy, it was a symbol of love, and young women would place pots of basil on their balconies to signal their availability for courtship.

Calla Lily

Zantedeschia aethiopica (Family: Araceae)

Light	Water	Temparature	Humidity	Pets
Ideal: Partial sun Tolerate: Full sun, Full shade	Every Week	65-75°F (18-24°C)	High (60-80%)	Not Safe for Cats and Dogs

CARING GUIDE

Water: Water on an average of once weekly, keep the soil around the plants moist but not soggy, and cut back in winter.

Light: Thrives in areas with moderate sunlight, can also adapt to full exposure to sun rays or complete shading. Inadequate sunlight may adversely affect its growth.

Fertilization: Dig compost into the soil once yearly in spring, and fertilize your once a month using an all-purpose fertilizer.

SUITABLE FOR:

Bedroom, Bathroom, Living Room, Balcony/Patio, East or North-facing window

Also known as: Arum lily

The Calla Lily, a true gem of the floral world, has graced homes and gardens for ages. This elegant beauty boasts award-winning cultivars like 'Crowborough,' 'Green Goddess,' 'Pink Mist,' and 'Red Desire.' Prized for both its cut flower elegance and vibrant garden presence. Its sturdy roots anchor it to the earth, while its graceful blooms reach towards the sun, a symbol of enduring charm.

Calla Lily, known scientifically as Zantedeschia aethiopica, is a species of flowering plant in the family Araceae, native to southern Africa in South Africa and Swaziland. The name "Calla" comes from the Greek word "kallos," which means beautiful. The specific epithet "aethiopica" refers to its southern African origin, not Ethiopia, as often assumed. The genus name "Zantedeschia" is in honor of Italian botanist Giovanni Zantedeschi. It's also commonly known as arum lily, and in some regions, it's known as the funeral flower due to its common use in funeral arrangements. Calla Lily was introduced to Europe in the mid-17th century. It gained popularity quickly due to its striking appearance and ease of cultivation.

CAPE JASMINE
Gardenia jasminoides (Family: Rubiaceae)

☀ LIGHT	💧 WATER	🌡 TEMPARATURE	◐ HUMIDITY	🪴 PETS
Ideal: Partial sun Tolerate: Full sun, Full shade	Every 1-2 weeks	60-80°F (15-27°C)	High (60-80%)	Not Safe for Cats and Dogs

Also known as: Cape jessamine, Gardenia

The gardenia jasminoides is an evergreen shrub that blends stunning flowers with unique, glossy leaves. Its exquisite, matte white blossoms, often gracing elegant bouquets, have captivated the hearts of gardeners and horticulturalists alike, earning it a place of adoration among ornamental plants. Its rich fragrance, reminiscent of a moonlit garden, adds an enchanting touch to any space.

Cape jasmine (Gardenia jasminoides) is native to the tropical regions of Africa, southern Asia, Australasia, and Oceania. The genus 'Gardenia' was named in honor of Dr. Alexander Garden (1730–1791), a Scottish-born American naturalist. The species name 'jasminoides' refers to its jasmine-like fragrance. It's commonly known as Cape Jasmine or Cape Jessamine, derived from its widespread cultivation in the Cape of Good Hope region of South Africa and its jasmine-like fragrance. In Japan, gardenia flowers were used to make a yellow dye for clothes and food. The flowers are also used in Chinese herbal medicine to treat various ailments, including insomnia, inflammation, and anxiety.

CARING GUIDE

Water: It likes moisture but doesn't like soggy soil. Requires regular watering, don't let the soil dry out completely.

Light: The optimal light exposure is a steady mix of sun and shade, with more emphasis on the latter. It can, however, endure whole day sunshine or stay in full shade.

Fertilization: Fertilize your Cape Jasmine monthly during spring, summer and fall using a balanced fertilizer or organic food.

SUITABLE FOR: Living Room, Balcony/Patio, South or West-facing window

COMMON LANTANA
Lantana camara (FAMILY: Verbenaceae)

LIGHT	WATER	TEMPERATURE	HUMIDITY	PETS
Ideal: Full sun Tolerate: Partial sun	Every 1-2 weeks	65-80°F (18-27°C)	Moderate (40-60%)	Not Safe for Cats and Dogs

CARING GUIDE

Water: Should be watered regularly, but avoid overwatering. Watered after the top two inches of soil are allowed to dry.

Light: Prefers abundant sunlight throughout the day, ro promote growth. It is also resilient and can remain healthy in areas where sunlight isn't as copious.

Fertilization: A balanced 20-20-20 NPK liquid fertilizer can be applied monthly during the growing season for best results.

SUITABLE FOR:
Balcony/Patio, South or West-facing window

Also known as: Lantana, Common Lantana, Shrub Verbena

Step aside, ordinary houseplants; the lantana's here to steal the spotlight! This charmer isn't just a garden darling - its vibrant flower clusters have taken the indoor jungle by storm. Even small lantanas put on a stunning show in a sunny window, showering you with endless blooms. This beauty is practically low-maintenance. Just give it enough sunshine and a sip of water now and then.

Common lantana (Lantana camara) is a species of flowering plant from the Verbena family, native to the American tropics. The genus name "Lantana" is thought to derive from the Latin name of the tree, Viburnum lantana, due to the similar appearance of their flowers. The species name "camara" comes from Greek, meaning "arched," "chambered," or "vaulted." The Latin word "lantana," meaning "a plant that grows and spreads quickly," fits due to the plant's rapid growth and spreading ability. Historically, Lantana camara spread from its native American tropics to around 50 countries, including Europe, Asia, and Oceania. It was first spread out of the Americas when Dutch explorers brought it to Europe.

COOPER'S HAWORTHIA
Haworthia cooperi (FAMILY: Asphodelaceae)

LIGHT	WATER	TEMPERATURE	HUMIDITY	PETS
Ideal: Full sun Tolerate: Partial sun	Every 2 weeks	50-70°F (10-21°C)	Moderate (40-50%)	Safe for Cats and Dogs

Also known as: Window Haworthia, Bristle Haworthia

Cooper's Haworthia is the South African beauty with attitude! This little succulent grows in tight clusters, like a spiky, emerald party huddled together. A homebody who prefers bright, indirect light and a good, long drink now and then. No need to be needy, after all! If you're looking for a low-maintenance cutie with a touch of South African sass, Cooper's your guy.

Haworthia cooperi, native to South Africa and specifically found in the Eastern Cape Province, is named in homage to Adrian Hardy Haworth, an English entomologist and botanist renowned for being among the first to study succulent plants. The species epithet, "cooperi," is a tribute to the contributions of Thomas Cooper, an English botanist and plant explorer who collected plants in South Africa between 1859 and 1862. These succulents, celebrated for their resilience and capacity to flourish in challenging environments, carry a symbolism. Planting succulents is often seen as a representation of endurance, strength, and other positive attributes, emphasizing their cultural and ornamental significance.

CARING GUIDE

Water: Water cooperi moderately. Make sure the soil is parched in between waterings. Excess water must be well-drained.

Light: Flourishes when exposed to substantial sunlight. It also copes under softer sun rays. Extensive light exposure accelerates its growth and vitality.

Fertilization: Doesn't need, replacing your plant's potting soil once a year should provide them with more than enough nutrition.

SUITABLE FOR:
Bedroom, Kitchen, Living Room, Office/Study Room, Balcony/Patio, East or North-facing window

COMMON SAGE
Salvia officinalis (FAMILY: Lamiaceae)

☀️ LIGHT	💧 WATER	🌡️ TEMPERATURE	💧 HUMIDITY	🐾 PETS
Ideal: Full sun Tolerate: Partial sun	Every Week	50-75°F (10-24°C)	Moderate (30-50%)	Safe for Cats and Dogs

Also known as: Garden Sage, True Sage, Dalmatian Sage

A beautiful evergreen, known as common sage, thrives in dry, rocky spots. It's been a culinary companion and beloved for its unique scent for centuries. Imagine candles, potpourri, and even beauty products infused with its lemony aroma! And let's not forget those gorgeous purple flowers that grace gardens and windowsills everywhere, adding a touch of the Mediterranean right to your home.

Common sage (Salvia officinalis) is part of the mint family, Lamiaceae, and is natively found in the Mediterranean region. The word "sage" in common sage comes from the Old French "sauge," which is derived from the Latin word "salvia." The root of this Latin term, "salvere," means "to save" or "to heal," reflecting the herb's early reputation for medicinal properties. The term "officinalis" is a common Latin suffix for plants with a long history of medicinal

CARING GUIDE

Water: Common sage needs watering once a week in spring, summer, and fall depending on how hot it is but less in winter.

Light: Thrives under plentiful exposure to the sun, and tolerates a lesser degree. Both extreme lack or excess may influencing its healthy growth negatively.

Fertilization: Aren't heavy feeders, and too much causes a weaker flavor. Use organic fertilizer for edible plants in the spring.

SUITABLE FOR: Kitchen, Living Room, Office/Study Room, Balcony/Patio, Children's Room, South or West-facing window

use. In ancient cultures, sage was often associated with immortality. This belief perhaps originated from its widespread medicinal use and its ability to preserve meat, suggesting a power to stave off decay and death. The Greeks and Romans considered sage a sacred herb, bestowing it with a status that required special rituals for its harvest. The Romans also used it in religious ceremonies, believing it could cleanse a space of evil. During the times of plague in medieval Europe, a mixture known as "Four Thieves Vinegar," which reportedly included sage, was believed to protect against the disease. The lore goes that four thieves were able to steal from the houses of plague victims without falling ill themselves, thanks to this herbal mixture. Sage has been used in various cultures for purification rituals. Burning sage -a practice that continues to this day- was believed to cleanse a space of evil spirits and negative energies, a tradition rooted in ancient practices.

Desert Rose
Adenium obesum (Family: Apocynaceae)

☀ LIGHT	💧 WATER	🌡 TEMPARATURE	💧 HUMIDITY	⚠ PETS
Ideal: Full sun Tolerate: Partial sun	Every 3 weeks	65-80°F (18-27°C)	Low (20-40%)	Not Safe for Cats and Dogs

CARING GUIDE

Water: Desert rose is a drought-tolerant plant. During the growing season, it will benefit from a steady supply of water.

Light: Thrives under the scorching rays that imitate its native desert dwelling. Strong illumination supports robust growth, though a level of shade can be tolerated.

Fertilization: During the growing season, desert rose should be fertilized once a month, with a slow-release 13-13-13 fertilizer.

SUITABLE FOR:
Balcony/Patio, South or West-facing window

Also known as: Mock Azalea, Impala Lily, Sabi Star

Often adored for its captivating blooms, the desert rose is a popular choice for indoor gardens. This resilient survivor, native to the arid landscapes of the Sahara, tropical Africa, and Arabia, thrives in warm climates, requiring temperatures no lower than 10°C. Remarkably, its sap has historically been used to coat arrowheads in Africa, a testament to its versatility and resourcefulness.

The Desert Rose, scientifically known as Adenium obesum, is a striking and unique plant known for its beautiful flowers and distinctive, swollen stem. The name "Adenium" is derived from "Aden," a region in Yemen, reflecting the plant's natural habitat in the Arabian Peninsula. The species name "obesum" comes from the Latin word for "obese," referring to the plant's swollen stem or caudex, a key characteristic of the species. The plant's caudex (swollen stem) is a fascinating adaptation for water storage, allowing it to survive in arid conditions. Adenium obesum is popular among bonsai enthusiasts. Its natural structure and ability to be shaped make it ideal for bonsai cultivation.

DILL
Anethum graveolens (FAMILY: Apiaceae)

LIGHT	WATER	TEMPERATURE	HUMIDITY	PETS
Ideal: Full sun Tolerate: partial sun	Twice per week	65-75°F (18-24°C)	Moderate (50-60%)	Safe for Cats and Dogs

Also known as: Dill Weed, Garden Dill, Sowa

This feathery friend is more than just a garnish! Dill struts its stuff with delicate leaves, ready to add its unique flavor punch to your culinary creations. Whether dried for later or snipped fresh, this herb has been a kitchen hero for ages - its history goes back all the way to Egyptian tombs! And in North America? It's the secret weapon that makes dill pickles so irresistible.

Dill (Anethum graveolens) is an aromatic herb known for its delicate, feathery leaves and distinctive flavor. The word "dill" comes from the Old English "dylle," likely derived from a Norse word meaning to soothe or lull, reflecting its traditional use as a carminative. "Graveolens" in Latin means "strong-smelling," which is a nod to the herb's potent aroma. Dill was often grown in monastery gardens and used by monks for its medicinal properties. It also featured in many folk remedies. In traditional Indian medicine, dill was used for its carminative properties, helping to alleviate gas and digestive issues. The Ebers Papyrus, an ancient Egyptian medical document, mentions dill as a soothing pain remedy.

CARING GUIDE

Water: While most herbs prefer drying, dill needs consistent watering. Water when the top inch of the pot soil feels dry.

Light: Dill thrives in areas abundant with sunlight exposure. Light requirement is key for its robust growth. Its natural habitat has similar light conditions

Fertilization: The indoor Dill plant needs more regular care, fertilize with a half-strength liquid fertilizer every 4-6 weeks.

SUITABLE FOR: Kitchen, Living Room, Office/Study Room, Balcony/Patio, Children's Room, South or West-facing window

Evergreen Azalea

Rhododendron indicum (Family: Ericaceae)

☀ LIGHT	💧 WATER	🌡 TEMPARATURE	％ HUMIDITY	✨ PETS
Ideal: Partial sun Tolerate: Full sun	Every 1-2 weeks	60-70°F (15-21°C)	High (60-80%)	Not Safe for Cats and Dogs

CARING GUIDE

Water: Quite drought-tolerant, though regular watering promotes blooming. Wilted leaves means your azalea needs water.

Light: Prefers areas where the sun filters through for most of the day, although it can tolerate more intense luminosity. Excessive radiation may lead to leaf burn.

Fertilization: Should be fertilized during the growing season with a slow-release fertilizer made specifically for rhododendrons.

SUITABLE FOR:
Balcony/Patio, East or North-facing window

Also known as: Tsutsusi azalea

The evergreen azalea is a robust and leafy shrub with a striking presence. It features magnificent cerise pink flowers with everlasting foliage. This plant prefers well-drained soils in partial shade because it has a low tolerance to wet soils, drought, and immoderate fertilizer. The overall components of the plant are ideal for decoration, but it is toxic and should not be used for consumption.

The Evergreen azalea (Rhododendron indicum) is a semi-evergreen plant in the Ericaceae (blueberry) family. The genus name Rhododendron derives from the Greek words rhodo, which means rose, and dendron, meaning tree. While "indicum" might suggest Indian origins, it's a historical misnomer. Upon encountering the azalea in trade routes with Asia, European botanists mistakenly assumed it hailed from India, hence the Latin epithet. However, the evergreen azalea proudly calls Japan its native land. Many varieties of Evergreen azaleas boast a delightful fragrance, adding an olfactory dimension to their aesthetic appeal. The sweet and sometimes spicy scent can transform a garden into a sensory delight.

FALSE SHAMROCK
Oxalis triangularis (Family: Oxalidaceae)

LIGHT	WATER	TEMPERATURE	HUMIDITY	PETS
Ideal: Partial sun Tolerate: Full sun, Full shade	Every Week	55-70°F (13-21°C)	Moderate (40-60%)	Not Safe for Cats and Dogs

Also known as: Wood Sorrel, Shamrock, Purple Shamrock

From the vibrant landscapes of South America emerges the false shamrock, a captivating houseplant that steals the show with its unique beauty. Its three-lobed leaves, not quite shamrocks but close enough to earn the name, with a captivating purple hue. Though this edible gem can add a zesty touch to your salad, remember to savor it in small bites, as its oxalic acid packs a hidden punch.

False Shamrock (Oxalis triangularis) is native to South America. The genus name "Oxalis" comes from the Greek word "oxys," meaning "sour," referring to the plant's sour-tasting leaves. The species name "triangularis" describes the shape of its leaves, which are notably triangular. The term "shamrock" refers to several small-leaved clovers, mainly the species Trifolium repens. The "false" prefix in "False Shamrock" is used because Oxalis triangularis is often mistaken for these clovers due to its similar three-leafed appearance. While not a true shamrock, it's often associated with the general symbolism of shamrock, which includes ideas of luck and prosperity, mainly due to its resemblance to the Irish shamrock.

CARING GUIDE

Water: Needs occasional deep watering. Water thoroughly until drainage, and wait until the soil dries before repeating.

Light: Prefers moderate exposure to sunlight, and able to tolerate full shade or abundant sunlight conditions. Too little or too much sun can disrupt its well-being.

Fertilization: Should only be fertilized during the spring and summer growing season. A balanced houseplant fertilizer is ideal.

SUITABLE FOR:
Bedroom, Bathroom, Kitchen, Living Room, Office/Study Room, Balcony/Patio, East or North-facing window

Fiddle Leaf Fig

Ficus lyrata (Family: Moraceae)

LIGHT	WATER	TEMPARATURE	HUMIDITY	PETS
Ideal: Partial sun Tolerate: Full sun, Full shade	Every 1-2 weeks	65-77°F (18-25°C)	Moderate (40-60%)	Not Safe for Cats and Dogs

CARING GUIDE

Water: Should be watered weekly in a well-drained pot. Overwatering and underwatering can cause grow issues.

Light: Flourishes under moderate sunlight. Though it adapts to a good or scant amount of sunlight, prefers a balanced amount, too much can scorch the leaves.

Fertilization: Can be fertilized using a 3-1-2 NPK liquid fertilizer. To avoid overfertilization, dilute the fertilizer by half.

SUITABLE FOR: Living Room, South or West-facing window

Also known as: Banjo Fig, Lyre Fig

The fiddle-leaf fig boasts leaves that gracefully mimic the shape of a violin. This widely adored houseplant makes a bold architectural statement with its unique and lush foliage. However, before welcoming this finicky beauty into your home, remember that it can be challenging to keep alive. This delicate plant demands well-draining soil and consistent humidity to thrive.

The Fiddle Leaf Fig, known scientifically as Ficus lyrata, is a species of flowering plant in the Moraceae family, native to western Africa, from Cameroon to Sierra Leone. The name "fiddle-leaf fig" comes from the shape of its leaves, which are broad at the apex and narrow in the middle, resembling a fiddle. Like other fig trees, Fiddle Leaf Figs have a rich presence in folklore across various cultures. In Roman mythology, the roots of a fig tree saved Romulus and Remus from drowning in the River Tiber. Ancient Egyptian pharaohs believed that when they were on their way to heaven, they would come across a fig tree at the edge of the desert, and the goddess Hathor would appear from the tree's foliage to greet them.

GHOST PLANT
Graptopetalum paraguayense (FAMILY: Crassulaceae)

☀ **LIGHT**	🪴 **WATER**	🌡 **TEMPARATURE**	💧 **HUMIDITY**	🐾 **PETS**
Ideal: Full sun Tolerate: Partial sun	Every 3 weeks	60-75°F (15-24°C)	Moderate (40-50%)	Safe for Cats and Dogs

Also known as: Mother-of-Pearl Plant, Mother of pearl

Meet the ghost plant, the succulent with a chameleon secret! This sun-kissed cutie hails from Mexico and rocks trailing rosettes that change color like magic. They bloom a soft yellow-pink in the sunshine, but it chills out with cool greenish-blueish-gray shades in the shade. Don't get it confused with its lookalike cousin, Echeveria - this ghost plant has a whole personality.

The Ghost Plant is native to Tamaulipas, Mexico. In its earlier taxonomic days, the plant went by the name Sedum weinbergii, an homage to the German botanist Gustav Weinberg. However, it was reclassified as Graptopetalum paraguayense. This name comes from the Greek words "grapto," meaning "painted" or "inscribed," and "petalon," meaning "petal." This name likely refers to the distinctive markings or colors found on the petals of plants in this genus. This adjustment in nomenclature reflects the ongoing refinement in our comprehension of plant taxonomy. The term "Ghost Plant" likely originates from the plant's pale or translucent appearance, which gives it a ghostly or ethereal look.

CARING GUIDE

Water: Prefers infrequent watering, water only when the soil is completely dry and the leaves become soft to the touch.

Light: Enjoys places with ample sunlight, thriving well under clear skies. However, it can also survive in less luminous spots. Inadequate light leads to faded leaves.

Fertilization: You can apply small amounts of general-purpose fertilizer during the active growing season but don't overfertilize.

SUITABLE FOR: Living Room, Office/Study Room, Balcony/Patio, Children's Room, South or West-facing window

Garden Marigold
Calendula officinalis (FAMILY: Asteraceae)

LIGHT	WATER	TEMPARATURE	HUMIDITY	PETS
Ideal: Full sun	Every	65-75°F	Moderate	Safe for Cats
Tolerate: Partial sun	Week	(18-24°C)	(50-60%)	and Dogs

Also known as: Pot Marigold, Calendula, Ruddles

Meet the pot marigold; this cheerful beauty boasts thick, orange-yellow blooms that burst with petals like a tiny fireworks display. But it's not just a beauty; it's a multi-talented MVP. Sprinkle its petals into your salad for a pop of color and zing, or use them to whip up a pot of sunshine-hued dye for your clothes or makeup. This plant's got a long history of gracing tables.

The genus name "Calendula" means the first day of the month, derived from the Latin word "kalendae," referring to the plant's long flowering period. "Officinalis" indicates its historical use in apothecaries and herbalism. The common name "Marigold" is believed to stem from "Mary's gold," a reference to the Virgin Mary in Christian tradition. This association may be due to the flower's use in early religious festivals. They were used in various religious ceremonies

CARING GUIDE

Water: Water once a week, when the soil surface dries. Give a good soaking but make sure that the soil drains thoroughly.

Light: Thrives when exposed to a generous amount of light daily. It tolerates conditions with slightly less light, though optimum growth is achieved with sun exposure.

Fertilization: Pot marigold doesn't require a fertilizer to thrive. Adding a phosphorous-rich fertilizer will encourage flowering.

SUITABLE FOR:
Kitchen, Living Room, Office/Study Room, Balcony/Patio, Children's Room, South or West-facing window

and were believed to possess protective qualities. In ancient times, marigolds were associated with the sun due to their bright color. The Egyptians valued them for their rejuvenating properties. In Hindu culture, marigolds have been used in religious ceremonies and weddings, symbolizing surrender to the divine. In Mexico, marigolds are known as "cempasúchil" and are used extensively during the Day of the Dead celebrations. They are believed to guide the spirits of the dead back to the world of the living due to their vibrant colors and strong fragrance. In medieval Europe, it was a common sight in herb gardens and was used for both culinary and medicinal purposes, including treating skin ailments and as an anti-inflammatory agent. Their petals, known for their slightly peppery taste, are used as a colorful addition to salads, soups, and baked goods. They are sometimes used as a natural food coloring, offering a golden hue to dishes.

HIBISCUS
Hibiscus rosa-sinensis (Family: Malvaceae)

☀ LIGHT	💧 WATER	🌡 TEMPARATURE	◌ HUMIDITY	🐾 PETS
Ideal: Full sun Tolerate: Partial sun	Every 1-2 weeks	55-75°F (13-24°C)	Moderate (50-60%)	Safe for Cats and Dogs

CARING GUIDE

Water: It's important to water the plant regularly, ensuring the soil remains evenly moist but not waterlogged.

Light: Prefers constant, unabated sunlight exposure and can endure slightly less sunny conditions. If provided an inadequate amount of light, its growth deteriorates.

Fertilization: Fertilize often (once a month), but lightly. A standard, balanced fertilizer will probably be sufficient.

SUITABLE FOR: Living Room, Balcony/Patio, Children's Room, South or West-facing window

Also known as: Shoeflower, Chinese hibiscus, China rose.

This evergreen shrub or small tree dazzles with funnel-shaped flowers that are typically red but can also be pink, orange, yellow, or white, like a fireworks show in your living room. This "China rose" actually likely originates from Southeast Asia, though some authorities point to Vanuatu in Oceania. It's so tough and bloomy that people worldwide fell in love.

Hibiscus (Hibiscus rosa-sinensis), commonly known as Chinese hibiscus, China rose, or Hawaiian hibiscus, belongs to the family Malvaceae. The common name "Hibiscus" is derived from the Greek word "hibiskos," referring to a mallow-like plant related to Hibiscus. The species name "rosa-sinensis" translates to "rose of China," indicating the plant's perceived origin and rose-like appearance. One of the most noted uses of Hibiscus rosa-sinensis in traditional medicine is for hair care. The flowers and leaves are often used in hair treatments to promote growth, prevent hair fall, and treat dandruff. The flowers are also used for their astringent properties in skin care, helping cleanse and tone the skin.

HINDU ROPE
Hoya compacta (Family: Apocynaceae)

☀️ LIGHT	💧 WATER	🌡️ TEMPARATURE	💧 HUMIDITY	🐾 PETS
Ideal: Full sun Tolerate: Partial sun	Every 3 weeks	60-80°F (15-27°C)	Moderate (50-60%)	Safe for Cats and Dogs

Also known as: Krinkle Kurl, Wax Plant, Porcelain Flower

A cascading curtain of lush emerald curls, all shiny and happy, that's the Hindu Rope, your green waterfall for your home! Forget boring vines – this beauty's like nature's own perm, bringing a touch of the unexpected jungle to your indoor oasis and thriving with just a bit of light and love. So, if you're looking for a unique and easygoing plant, the Hindu Rope is your new best friend.

The Hindu Rope plant, known scientifically as Hoya compacta, has never been observed in the wild; perhaps it is the result of experimental work by a plant-loving alchemist. The genus name "Hoya" is a tribute to Thomas Hoy, an English gardener and botanist in the late 18th century, known for his work with the Duke of Northumberland at Syon House. This Latin word translates to "compact" or "dense." It aptly describes the Hoya compacta's growth habit, characterized by tightly clustered, twisted leaves that grow close together on its vines. The sweet scent of the Hoya compacta flowers is most pronounced at night, a characteristic thought to attract nocturnal pollinators in its natural habitat.

CARING GUIDE

Water: Does not tolerate overwatering. If your pot drain well, and you don't water too often, you should be pretty safe.

Light: Prefers a consistent sunlight and can also manage well in areas where sunlight filters in heterogeneously. Persistent excessive sunlight may lead to leaf scorch.

Fertilization: During the spring and summer only, fertilize monthly or so with a gentle liquid fertilizer like Indoor Plant Food.

SUITABLE FOR:
Bedroom, Bathroom, Kitchen, Living Room, Office/Study Room, Children's Room, East or North-facing window

Horseshoe Geranium

Pelargonium zonale (Family: Geraniaceae)

Light	Water	Temparature	Humidity	Pets
Ideal: Full sun Tolerate: Partial sun	Every Week	50-70°F (10-21°C)	Moderate (40-60%)	Not Safe for Cats and Dogs

CARING GUIDE

Water: Requires infrequent, deep watering. Allow the soil to dry out between waterings and water thoroughly when dried.

Light: Thrives in abundant sunlight, and can endure less direct light. Hailing from sun-drenched territories, Its health is inextricably connected to abundant sunlight.

Fertilization: During the growing season, fertilize this plant every two weeks. Use liquid, general-purpose, balanced fertilizer.

SUITABLE FOR: Kitchen, Living Room, Balcony/Patio, Children's Room, South or West-facing window

Also known as: Geranium, zonal pelargonium

Easily recognizable by the horseshoe-shaped patterns, horseshoe geraniums boast delightful blooms that attract bees, butterflies, and birds. These vibrant blossoms come in a lovely spectrum of colors, including red and pink, adding a touch of charm to any outdoor yard or indoor container garden. Abundant blooms and easy care make horseshoe geraniums a favorite among gardeners.

Horseshoe geranium, scientifically known as Pelargonium zonale, is native to South Africa and was introduced to Europe in the 17th century. Their popularity in horticulture grew rapidly in the 18th and 19th centuries, especially in England. The scientific name "Pelargonium" comes from the Greek word 'Pelargos' meaning "stork," referring to the beak-like shape of the seedpod. "Zonale" derives from the Latin "zonale", indicative of the zoned pattern often found on the leaves, and the common name "Horseshoe geranium" likely originates from the horseshoe-shaped markings on the leaves. Geraniums have been used symbolically in various cultures, often representing comfort, health, or good fortune.

KENTIA PALM
Howea forsteriana (FAMILY: Arecaceae)

LIGHT	**WATER**	**TEMPARATURE**	**HUMIDITY**	**PETS**
Ideal: Full sun Tolerate: Partial sun	Every 1-2 weeks	65-80°F (18-27°C)	Moderate (40-50%)	Safe for Cats and Dogs

Also known as: Sentry Palm, Paradise Palm, Thatch Palm

The Kentia palm is a marvelous palm tree well-suited to tropical climates and a popular choice for indoor decor. While it grows slowly, it can become quite tall. Its elegant fronds are arching and feather-like with lush green leaves that extend from a slender trunk, which matures in color over time. Toward the end of the year, it produces creamy white flowers, followed by small fruits.

The Kentia Palm (Howea forsteriana) is a species of palm native to Lord Howe Island in Australia. The palm's genus name, Howea, derives from the palm's native location, Lord Howe Island. The species name "forsteriana" honors William Forster, a prominent political figure in New South Wales during the 19th century. Locally, on Lord Howe Island, the Ketia Palm's fronds were used for thatching and in various crafts. The Kentia Palm is also known as the "Sentry Palm" because it was used as a decorative plant in the entrance halls of Victorian homes. The Kentia Palm was a favorite in royal courts. It's said that Queen Victoria was particularly fond of these palms, and they were a staple in many of her royal residences.

CARING GUIDE

Water: Prefers regular watering, but it doesn't tolerate waterlogged soil. Water the plant when the soil has dried out.

Light: Kentia palm favours substantial exposure to the sun for optimal growth. Lack of adequate sunlight could stunt its growth, while too much can burn the leaves.

Fertilization: Fertilize once a month during the growing season, in spring and summer. Apply all-purpose, slow-release fertilizer.

SUITABLE FOR:
Bedroom, Bathroom, Kitchen, Living Room, Balcony/Patio, Children's Room, East or North-facing window

Lemon Balm
Melissa officinalis (FAMILY: Lamiaceae)

LIGHT	WATER	TEMPARATURE	HUMIDITY	PETS
Ideal: Full sun Tolerate: Partial sun	Every Week	60-70°F (15-21°C)	Moderate (50-60%)	Safe for Cats and Dogs

Also known as: Bee Balm, Sweet Balm, Common Balm

Lemon balm's not just pretty with a calming scent – its essential oils are like tiny sunshine bombs, adding a citrusy kick to perfumes, soaps, and even your homemade cleaning spray. This happy herbaceous friend loves buzzing with bees and basking in the sun. People have been smitten with its lemony goodness since the 16th century! So go ahead and give your home a sniff of sunshine.

Lemon Balm has historical connections to ancient civilizations. In Greek mythology, the plant is said to have been named after the Greek nymph Melissa, who was transformed into a bee after she died. The plant was believed to have been created by the goddess Diana to feed her sacred bees. The Greeks and Romans valued it for its medicinal properties and used it to make perfumes and bathwater. In medieval times, it found its way into monastery gardens; It was thought to

CARING GUIDE

Water: Water the plant deeply as soon as it begins to look wilted. Timings can vary depending on the plant's location.

Light: Thrives when exposed to abundant sunlight throughout the day, though it can also get by in slightly shadowed spots. Too much sun may cause leaf scorching.

Fertilization: Prefers soil mulch rather than a fertilizer. This is because the delightful aroma is reduced by using fertilizers.

SUITABLE FOR:
Kitchen, Living Room, Office/Study Room, Balcony/Patio, Children's Room, South or West-facing window

ward off evil spirits and promote good fortune. In medieval times, Lemon Balm was often used to make a beverage called "Carmelite water" or "Melissa water." Monks in the Carmelite order were said to have used it in a tonic mixed with wine. The generic name "Melissa" is derived from the Greek word for honeybee. Lemon Balm has historically been associated with bees, and its sweet lemon fragrance is believed to attract these pollinators. The plant was often planted near beehives to encourage bee activity. Lemon Balm is used in the kitchen to impart a lemony flavor to dishes, salads, desserts, and teas. It pairs well with fish, chicken, and fruit salads. Lemon Balm tea is a common herbal infusion known for its calming properties. It is often consumed to promote relaxation and alleviate stress. The essential oil extracted from Lemon Balm is used in cosmetic products for its pleasant fragrance. It is also included in some perfumes and skincare items.

LIVING STONES
Lithops (Family: Aizoaceae)

LIGHT	**WATER**	**TEMPARATURE**	**HUMIDITY**	**PETS**
Ideal: Full sun	Every	60-80°F	Moderate	Safe for Cats
Tolerate: Partial sun	3 weeks	(15-27°C)	(40-50%)	and Dogs

CARING GUIDE

Water: Water from late spring into summer by using the 'soak and dry' method. Takecare, overwatering can lead to root rot.

Light: Thrives under generous sunlight exposure. Throughout its growth, whether in budding or mature stages, substantial sunlight enhances its health.

Fertilization: Lithops do not need much fertilization as it may cause damage. Being native to soils containing very few nutrients.

SUITABLE FOR:
Balcony/Patio, Children's Room, South or West-facing window

Also known as: Stone Plants, Flowering Stones

Living stone plants are masters of disguise, practically akin to chameleons in the plant world. Their plump, fleshy leaves are expertly shaped to mimic smooth stones, deceiving the eye and blending seamlessly into their surroundings. These little tricksters are stars in the houseplant community, offering a unique and low-maintenance option for plant enthusiasts.

Living Stones (Lithops) is native to Namibia and South Africa. The name "Living Stones" is derived from their stone-like appearance. These plants have evolved to mimic the rocks among which they grow to avoid being eaten by herbivores. The genus name "Lithops" comes from the Greek words "lithos" (meaning stone) and "ops" (meaning face), indicating the stone-like appearance of the plants. There are 37 recognized species of Lithops, along with numerous varieties. This diversity is a result of their adaptation to various microhabitats and specific ecological niches. These plants are a prime example of evolutionary adaptation. Their ability to blend in with their surroundings is a remarkable survival strategy.

MADAGASCAR DRAGON TREE
Dracaena marginata (Family: Asparagaceae)

☀ LIGHT	💧 WATER	🌡 TEMPARATURE	💧 HUMIDITY	🐾 PETS
Ideal: Full sun Tolerate: Partial sun	Every 2-3 weeks	60-80°F (15-27°C)	Moderate (40-60%)	Not Safe for Cats and Dogs

Also known as: Red-Edged Dracaena, Dragon Plant

The Madagascar dragon tree is a striking and charming houseplant that has stolen the hearts of many with its tri-colored leaves and graceful, slender stalks. Its vibrant green sword-like leaves edged in delicate white and blushing pink, add a touch of exotic elegance to any home. Renowned for its easygoing nature, this resilient, beloved plant thrives with minimal care.

The Madagascar Dragon Tree, scientifically known as Dracaena marginata, is native to Madagascar and is a member of the Asparagaceae family. The genus name "Dracaena" comes from the Greek word "drakaina", meaning "female dragon," referring to the bright red resin in the stems of some species that resembles dragon blood. The species name "marginata" is derived from Latin, meaning "bordered," likely referring to the plant's leaf distinctive red or purplish margins. NASA's Clean Air Study found that Dracaena marginata is effective in removing harmful chemicals like xylene, trichloroethylene, and formaldehyde from the air. This makes it not just a decorative addition but also beneficial for indoor air quality.

CARING GUIDE

Water: It's easy to over-water the drought-tolerant dragon tree. So, water only when the top half of the soil is dry.

Light: Prefers bright light and can tolerate partial shade. Plants kept in lower light situations will grow slower and produce smaller leaves with less intense color.

Fertilization: Doesn't need, but to boost growth, add a balanced controlled-release liquid fertilizer at the beginning of spring.

SUITABLE FOR:
Bedroom, Bathroom, Kitchen, Living Room, Office/Study Room, East or North-facing window

Madagascar Jasmine
Stephanotis floribunda (Family: Apocynaceae)

☀️ LIGHT	💧 WATER	🌡️ TEMPERATURE	% HUMIDITY	🐾 PETS
Ideal: Full sun Tolerate: partial sun	Every Week	65-75°F (18-24°C)	High (60-70%)	Safe for Cats and Dogs

CARING GUIDE

Water: Water when the top 3 cm of soil begins to dry out in spring and summer, then more sparingly in autumn and winter.

Light: Prefers moderate to abundant sunlight. It can tolerate places where the solar rays are more muted. Health can deteriorate if sunlight is too low or too high.

Fertilization: Feed every 2 weeks in spring and summer with a phosphorous or potassium-rich non-high-nitrogen liquid fertilizer.

SUITABLE FOR: Living Room, South or West-facing window

Also known as: Bridal Wreath, Waxflower

This captivating Madagascar jasmine will weave its way into your heart. Its large, glossy leaves, like emerald ovals, unfurl to an impressive 10 centimeters. Imagine clusters of waxy white stars, each a tiny perfume bottle, filling the air with their intoxicating sweetness. Bring it inside, bathe it in bright light, and it might just reward you with fragrant blossoms all year round.

The Madagascar Jasmine is a popular choice in wedding bouquets and floral arrangements. The name "Stephanotis floribunda" has Greek origins. The genus name "Stephanotis" is derived from the Greek words "Stephanos," meaning crown, and "otus," meaning ear. This name was given to the plant due to the unique structure of its flowers, which are arranged in clusters resembling a crown. It symbolizes marital happiness, fidelity, and the sweetness of love. Its delicate and fragrant flowers are often linked to the purity and beauty of a bride. In some cultures, the Madagascar Jasmine is associated with expressions of love and romance. The sweet fragrance of its blossoms adds to its reputation as a symbol of affection.

MAJESTY PALM
Ravenea rivularis (FAMILY: Arecaceae)

LIGHT	WATER	TEMPARATURE	HUMIDITY	PETS
Ideal: Full sun Tolerate: Partial sun	Every 2 weeks	65-80°F (18-27°C)	Moderate (40-50%)	Safe for Cats and Dogs

Also known as: Majestic Palm, Majestic Majesty

Imagine bringing a piece of Madagascar's rainforest right into your home. That's the magic of the Majesty Palm. This tropical stunner unfurls its emerald elegance like a living sculpture, its fronds gracefully arching toward the sun. Picture it basking in a sun-drenched corner, its deep green leaves shimmering like jewels. This air-purifying cleanses your breath and brightens your mood.

The Majesty Palm, scientifically known as Ravenea rivularis, is a popular plant known for its graceful, feathery fronds and easy adaptability to indoor environments. The common name "Majesty Palm" reflects its regal, majestic appearance, which makes it a favored ornamental plant. The genus name "Ravenea" is derived from the Malagasy word for palm, reflecting its origins in Madagascar. "Rivularis" comes from Latin, meaning 'of or pertaining to brooks or streams,' indicating its natural habitat near water sources. The Majesty Palm is often used in upscale hotels and resorts as a symbol of tropical luxury. Its lush foliage is associated with exotic and leisurely vacation destinations.

CARING GUIDE

Water: Need to allow the soil to dry out half way down between waterings. Expect to water more often in brighter light.

Light: Thrives in substantial sunlight, which is crucial for its health and growth. It can adapt to a less sunny environment. Overexposure can scorch the leaves.

Fertilization: A typical houseplant fertilizer with slightly higher nitrogen levels fed to your plant once a month will be enough.

SUITABLE FOR:
Bedroom, Bathroom, Kitchen, Living Room, Balcony/Patio, Children's Room, East or North-facing window

MEXICAN SNOW BALL

Echeveria elegans (FAMILY: Crassulaceae)

☀ LIGHT	💧 WATER	🌡 TEMPARATURE	◯% HUMIDITY	🐾 PETS
Ideal: Full sun	Every	65-75°F	Moderate	Safe for Cats
Tolerate: partial sun	3 weeks	(18-24°C)	(30-50%)	and Dogs

CARING GUIDE

Water: Water after the soil has been allowed to dry out completely. Completely soaking the substrate and then drain well.

Light: Has a preference for an environment saturated with sunlight. However, it can endure locations where the sun's rays are obstructed occasionally.

Fertilization: use a small amount of balanced or succulent-specific fertilizer if the soil is poor or the plant is struggling.

SUITABLE FOR: Living Room, Balcony/Patio, Children's Room, South or West-facing window

Also known as: Mexican gem, White Mexican Rose

The Mexican snowball is a superstar, ready to brighten any windowsill. It's not your typical drama queen – it craves sunshine and sips water like a champ. This little gem packs a punch with its plump, colorful leaves that change hues like a chameleon to match its mood. So, if you want to add a touch of whimsy to your indoor oasis, look no further than the Mexican snowball!

The common name "Mexican snowball" for Echeveria elegans likely derives from the plant's appearance. Echeveria elegans has pale blue-green leaves that are densely arranged, creating a spherical or ball-like shape. The soft, powdery coating on the leaves enhances the visual similarity to snow, hence the name "snowball.". The name "Echeveria elegans" was given to this succulent to honor a Mexican botanical artist named Atanasio Echeverría y Godoy. The genus name "Echeveria" is dedicated to him as a tribute to his contributions to the field of botanical illustration. Meanwhile, the species name "elegans" is derived from the Latin word meaning "elegant" or "graceful," which describes the plant's aesthetic qualities.

POINSETTIA
Euphorbia Pulcherrima (Family: Euphorbiaceae)

☼ LIGHT	🜄 WATER	🌡 TEMPARATURE	💧 HUMIDITY	🔧 PETS
Ideal: Full sun	Every	60-70°F	Moderate	Not Safe for
Tolerate: Partial sun	1-2 weeks	(15-21°C)	(50-60%)	Cats and Dogs

Also known as: Painted leaf, Mexican flame leaf

This beauty may hail from Mexico, but it has become the queen of Christmas in the US. Today, over 70 million poinsettias light up homes for just six magical weeks. Pass on the ordinary evergreens; this red-hot beauty is the only decor you need! It loves bright, indirect sunlight and thrives on a good soak now and then. It'll bring a touch of sunshine to even the gloomiest December day.

The Poinsettia (Euphorbia Pulcherrima) is named after Joel Poinsett, the first U.S. Ambassador to Mexico who introduced the plant to the United States in the early 19th century, the vibrant red and green leaves have become synonymous with the festive season. In Mexico, its native land, the Aztecs called it "Cuitlaxochitl," meaning "flower of the painted flames," and revered it for its medicinal properties. Legend tells of a poor girl who brought simple weeds as an offering to the Christ child, only for them to miraculously bloom into the first Poinsettias, symbolizing hope and humility. Today, its vibrant colors and association with Christmas continue to resonate, making it a cherished symbol of the season.

CARING GUIDE

Water: Check the surrounding soil, if it is dry, then water the plant deeply. Make sure it is grown in well-drained soil.

Light: Thrives under generous sunlight exposure. It can manage less exposure. Ample sunlight promote vibrant hues in poinsettia's red and green leaves.

Fertilization: Fertilize twice a year (6 weeks after blooming , and 6 weeks after this), using a balanced houseplant fertilizer.

SUITABLE FOR: South or West-facing window

ROSEMARY
Salvia rosmarinus (FAMILY: Lamiaceae)

☀️ LIGHT	💧 WATER	🌡️ TEMPERATURE	💧 HUMIDITY	🐾 PETS
Ideal: Full sun Tolerate: Partial sun	Every Week	55-75°F (13-24°C)	Moderate (30-50%)	Safe for Cats and Dogs

Also known as: Sea Dew, Compass Plant

This charming herb has soft, silvery-blue leaves and delicate pale flowers. For well over 7,000 years, it's been a trusted companion in kitchens and homes around the Mediterranean. Its distinctive, woodsy scent isn't just a delight for our noses; it's been woven into the fabric of life, gracing everything from roasts to refreshing soaps and candles. It's a time-traveling treasure.

The name "rosemary" originates from the Latin words "ros" (meaning 'dew') and "marinus" (meaning 'of the sea'), which together mean "dew of the sea." This name likely refers to its natural habitat along the Mediterranean coast, where it can often survive on just the humidity carried by the sea breeze. The scientific name 'Salvia rosmarinus' is a result of recent taxonomic changes. It has been reclassified under the genus Salvia. In Latin, "Salvia" derives from "salvare,"

CARING GUIDE

Water: Should be watered regularly and the top layer of surrounding soil should be allowed to dry out in between watering.

Light: Requires ample amount of light exposure. It can also endure places with less consistent light. Sufficient light fosters flowering and enhances scent production.

Fertilization: Feed using a liquid fertilizer at the start of its growing season (spring) and continuing monthly through the fall.

SUITABLE FOR:
Kitchen, Living Room, Office/Study Room, Balcony/Patio, Children's Room, South or West-facing window

meaning "to save" or "to heal," indicative of the plant's historical use in medicine. Rosemary was associated with Aphrodite/Venus, the goddess of love, who was said to be draped in it when she rose from the sea. The Egyptians used it in their burial rituals. The Greeks and Romans prized it for its medicinal properties and as a symbol of loyalty, love, and remembrance. Ancient Greek students would wear rosemary garlands around their heads while studying, believing it enhanced their memory. In Shakespeare's "Hamlet," Ophelia says, "There's rosemary, that's for remembrance; pray, love, remember." This line has immortalized the herb as a symbol of memory. It's said that Napoleon Bonaparte was particularly fond of rosemary and used water infused with the herb for bathing. He cultivated the herb at Malmaison, his residence, and reportedly used rosemary-infused eau de cologne and perfume.

Silver Dollar

Crassula arborescens (Family: Crassulaceae)

☀ LIGHT	💧 WATER	🌡 TEMPARATURE	◌ HUMIDITY	✻ PETS
Ideal: Full sun Tolerate: Partial sun	Every 3 weeks	65-75°F (18-24°C)	Moderate (40-60%)	Not Safe for Cats and Dogs

CARING GUIDE

Water: Drought-tolerant. Water this succulent thoroughly when dry out, then allow them to dry out before watering again.

Light: Craves a generous amount of sun exposure for healthy growth, akin to its original sun-drenched environment. It can endure in areas with less sunlight.

Fertilization: Simply fertilize with a small amount of organic compost in mid-spring when the silver dollar plant begins growing.

SUITABLE FOR: Living Room, Office/Study Room, Balcony/Patio, Children's Room, South or West-facing window

Also known as: Dollar Plant, Silver jade plant

Imagine a houseplant that's like a tiny, sparkling winter wonderland. Meet the silver dollar plant, a succulent shrub with round, silvery leaves that gleam like miniature coins. This beauty grows 61 to 122 cm tall and even puts on a show in winter, blooming with delicate white and pink flowers. It's a reminder that even in the coldest months, nature can surprise you with magic.

Silver Dollar (Crassula arborescens), also known as the Silver Jade Plant, is a succulent native to South Africa that grows in rocky outcrops and hillsides. It's part of the Crassulaceae family, which includes many other succulents. The name "Crassula" derives from the Latin word 'Crassus,' which means thick or fat, referring to the thick leaves of plants in this genus. The specific epithet 'arborescens' means tree-like, indicating its growth habit. The name "Silver Dollar" for Crassula arborescens likely originates from the appearance of the plant's unique foliage. The leaves of Crassula arborescens are typically round, flat, and silver-gray, resembling silver coins or, more specifically, old silver dollars.

STRING OF PEARLS
Curio rowleyanus (Family: Asteraceae)

Light
Ideal: Full sun
Tolerate: Partial sun

Water
Every
2-3 weeks

Temparature
60-75°F
(15-24°C)

Humidity
Moderate
(40-60%)

Pets
Not Safe for
Cats and Dogs

Also known as: String of Beads, Bead Plant, Rosary Plant

Picture a cascading waterfall of emerald beads, each one a tiny pearl. That's what the String of Pearls plant is like. Its delicate stems trail gracefully, with pea-sized leaves resembling a pearl strand. This enchanting succulent isn't just a visual delight; it also graces us with delicate blooms, their stamens bursting with vibrant hues, and a delightful cinnamon-like aroma.

The String of Pearls, scientifically known as Curio rowleyans, is a fascinating succulent that captivates gardeners and enthusiasts alike. Its name is derived from the bead-like leaves that cascade down the plant, resembling a delicate string of pearls. The plant is also known as "String of Tears," as its trailing tendrils are said to symbolize tears of joy. The genus name "Curio" is derived from the Latin word "curious," meaning "curious" or "interesting." It was chosen to reflect the fascinating appearance of the plant, with its cascading strings of pearl-like leaves. The species name, "Rowleyanus," honors the British botanist Gordon Douglas Rowley, who significantly contributed to the study of succulent plants.

CARING GUIDE

Water: Should never be overwatered, allow the soil to dry to fingernail depth between waterings. Water every 2-3 weeks.

Light: Favors ample light, a consequence of its native habitat. It's quite resilient to moderate sun exposure as well. Exposure to strong rays could harm its health.

Fertilization: Use no more than a diluted to half strength, balanced liquid fertilizer every few weeks during the growing season.

SUITABLE FOR:
Bedroom, Living Room, Office/Study Room, Balcony/Patio, West or South-facing window

Taro
Colocasia esculenta (FAMILY: Araceae)

LIGHT	WATER	TEMPERATURE	HUMIDITY	PETS
Ideal: Full sun Tolerate: Partial sun	Every Week	65-80°F (18-27°C)	High (60-80%)	Not Safe for Cats and Dogs

Also known as: Yam, Cocoyam, Dasheen, Elephant's Ear

The Taro plant, known for its large leaves, comes in lime green, purple, or black. It is a versatile perennial. While in warmer months, it can be planted outdoors, it's also well-suited for indoor environments, where it adds a tropical touch. It pairs beautifully with other exotic plants and thrives in moist soil, making it ideal for indoors or near ponds when grown outside.

The Taro plant "Colocasia esculenta" has a rich cultural and historical background. The term "taro" was borrowed from Māori during Captain Cook's observation of Colocasia plantations in New Zealand in 1769. Colocasia esculenta's specific epithet, "esculenta," means "edible" in Latin, referring to its use as a food source. In Hawaiian mythology, the taro is considered an ancestor of Hawaiians. The legend involves the deities Papahānaumoku (Earth

CARING GUIDE

Water: Requires constantly moist soil, so water it regularly as soon as the soil begins to dry out. It enjoys wet soils.

Fertilization: Needs to be fertilized during fall and winter. Apply a balanced liquid fertilizer with an N-P-K ratio of 10-10-10.

Light: Thrives in abundant sunlight, tolerating also partial shade. It needs adequate light to maintain its health, as insufficient sunlight can lead to stunted growth.

SUITABLE FOR:
Bathroom, South or West-facing window

mother) and Wākea (Sky father), who created the islands of Hawaii, and a woman, Hoʻohokukalani. Their child, Hāloanakalaukapalili, was stillborn, and a taro plant grew over his grave. The second child, Hāloa, named after his brother, was sustained by the kalo (taro) of the earth, making taro the principal food for generations. Taro has been a staple food in many regions, particularly the Pacific Islands, Asia, and Africa. Its corms and leaves are edible when cooked, providing a significant source of carbohydrates and nutrients. Taro is believed to have been cultivated for thousands of years. Archaeological evidence suggests its cultivation in ancient civilizations, possibly dating back to 5000 BCE or earlier in regions like India, Egypt, and China. The cultivation of taro in the Pacific Islands is linked with the history of Polynesian navigation. It was one of the staple crops carried by Polynesian voyagers as they explored and settled the Pacific.

THYME
Thymus vulgaris (FAMILY: Lamiaceae)

LIGHT	WATER	TEMPERATURE	HUMIDITY	PETS
Ideal: Full sun Tolerate: Partial sun	Every 1-2 weeks	50-75°F (10-24°C)	Moderate (30-50%)	Safe for Cats and Dogs

Also known as: Garden Thyme, Common Thyme, Lemon Thyme

This little thyme is a superstar herb that's as happy indoors as it is outside. It's a slow starter from seed, but once it gets going, it rewards you with a bounty of flavorful leaves on its upright, woody stems. In just one season, you can have a mini forest of thyme. Just grab some seeds and a potted nursery plant, and get ready to add a touch of the Mediterranean to your indoor jungle.

Thyme (Thymus vulgaris) is an herb known for its aromatic and culinary uses, as well as its role in traditional medicine. The word "thyme" originates from the Greek word "thymos," meaning "to fumigate" this refers to the smell generated by the burn of thyme as incense in ancient Greek temples, and "vulgaris" in Latin means "common," distinguishing this species as the most familiar or widespread among its genus. In ancient Egypt, thyme was used in

CARING GUIDE

Water: Thrives in dry, well-drained soil. Avoids soggy conditions, where it will rot. It should be watered to stay moist.

Light: Thrives in an environment that captures the full sunlight throughout the day, and also tolerates areas that offer a moderate level of solar exposure.

Fertilization: Doesn't need. If you want a boost, feed it with a diluted liquid organic fertilizer early on in its growing season

SUITABLE FOR:
Kitchen, Living Room, Office/Study Room, Balcony/Patio, Children's Room, South or West-facing window

the embalming process due to its strong preservative and antibacterial properties. The Greeks used it as a fumigant, believing it had purifying qualities. During the Black Death in Europe, thyme was included in recipes for "Four Thieves Vinegar," a concoction believed to protect against the plague. Thyme's antiseptic properties were employed during World War I. It was used in field dressings to prevent infection, acknowledging its medicinal value. In some European traditions, thyme was believed to be a favorite plant of fairies. It was thought that a patch of wild thyme was a sign that fairies had danced there. This folklore led to the tradition of including thyme in gardens to attract fairies. Beyond its basic culinary uses, thyme was historically important in various European cuisines for preserving and flavoring meats, especially before the advent of modern refrigeration techniques. It was also used in the making of liqueurs and herbal wines.

Venus Flytrap

Dionaea muscipula (Family: Droseraceae)

☼ LIGHT	💧 WATER	🌡 TEMPARATURE	% HUMIDITY	🐾 PETS
Ideal: Full sun Tolerate: partial sun	Twice per week	60-80°F (15-27°C)	Moderate (40-60%)	Safe for Cats and Dogs

CARING GUIDE

Water: Avoid watering from the top, place your Venus fly trap's pot into a small dish of rainwater or distilled water.

Light: Thrives best in natural, direct, outdoor sunlight. Exposure to full sunlight allows it to grow healthy and to its full size and display attractive coloration.

Fertilization: A very sensitive plant that is adapted to growing in poor-quality soils. This plant is best left to feed itself.

SUITABLE FOR: Living Room, Balcony/Patio, South or West-facing window

Also known as: Flytrap, Waterwheel Plant, Dionaea

The Venus flytrap isn't your average houseplant. This plant's got a taste for adventure. Instead of just soaking up the sun, it lures unsuspecting insects into its hinged jaws, which are actually modified leaves! Once those jaws snap shut, dinner's served. This plant's got a surprising appetite, all thanks to its clever disguise as a harmless flower. It's like a tiny Venus in a leafy trap.

The name "Venus Flytrap" blends mythology and botany. The name "Venus" refers to the goddess of love and beauty in Roman mythology, adding elegance to a species known for its interesting appearance. The scientific name Dionaea muscipula, chosen by John Ellis, further emphasizes the connection to beauty and love by translating to "daughter of Dione," the goddess Aphrodite. "Muscipula," Latin for "mousetrap," aptly describes the plant's unique mechanism. Charles Darwin explored the Venus Flytrap in "Insectivorous Plants," discussing its structure and evolutionary significance. The plant also appears in fiction, like the novel "Little Shop of Horrors" by Alan Menken and Howard Ashman, adding to its cultural significance.

Zebra Haworthia
Haworthia fasciata (Family: Asphodelaceae)

LIGHT	**WATER**	**TEMPARATURE**	**HUMIDITY**	**PETS**
Ideal: Full sun Tolerate: Partial sun	Every 3 weeks	50-70°F (10-21°C)	Moderate (30-50%)	Safe for Cats and Dogs

Also known as: Zebra Plant, Zebra Cactus, Pearl Plant

The zebra plant, the living sculpture with the stripes to prove it! Dark green leaves banded with pearly white, it's like a mini jungle in your home. This little charmer is as easygoing as they come. Pop it in a funky pot and watch it work its magic on tables, coffee nooks, or even your windowsill. It's the perfect touch of wildness wherever you need a little untamed beauty.

Its name "Haworthia," pays homage to the accomplished British botanist Adrian Hardy Haworth, while "fasciata" derives from the Latin word "fascia," meaning band or stripe, alluding to the distinctive zebra-like bands on its leaves. It is also commonly referred to as the "Pearl Plant" due to the unique appearance of its leaves. The leaves of Haworthia fasciata are characterized by translucent "windows" or "pearl-like" tips that allow sunlight to penetrate and reach the inner parts of the leaves. Legend has it that these succulents were believed to bring good luck and prosperity to the households that cultivated them. In folktale, the Zebra Haworthia was considered a protective charm, guarding against negative energies.

CARING GUIDE

Water: Requires infrequent, intense watering. Soak the soil and then wait until it has fully dried out before rewatering.

Light: Thrives under the generous intensity of the sun, although it can tolerate a moderate amount of sunlight. Adequate sunlight contributes to its healthy growth.

Fertilization: Use a liquid fertilizer for succulent plants no more than once every 2-3 months. Keep the soil slightly acidic.

SUITABLE FOR:
Bedroom, Kitchen, Living Room, Office/Study Room, Balcony/Patio, East or North-facing window

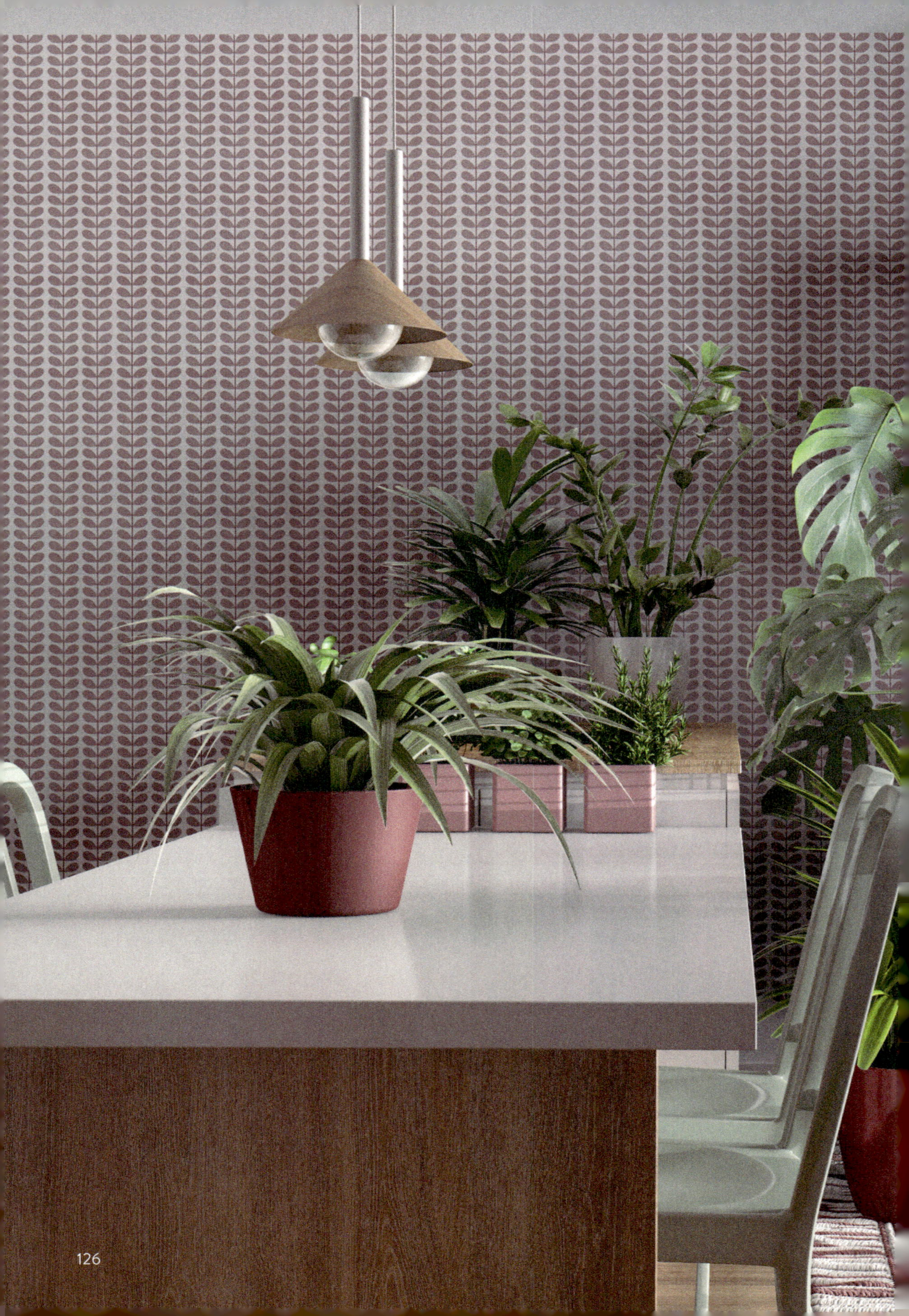

Section 4:
THE RIGHT PLANT FOR EVERY SPACE

Green Harmony: Tailoring Plants to Your Space and Lifestyle

"The Right Plant for Every Space" is a guide to selecting perfect plants for different areas of your home. It shows how to bring nature into your spaces, from bedrooms to balconies, by choosing plants that suit and enhance these environments. The guide helps align plant choices with your lifestyle, ensuring they grow well and enhance each space's qualities.

6
HOUSEPLANTS FOR BEGINNERS

Houseplant collections, perfect for beginners, thrive under irregular watering and varying light conditions. Suited for dorms, offices, or dim corners, these resilient and versatile plants brighten any space, offering an excellent option for those developing their gardening skills.

Golden Pothos

Adaptable vine thriving in various conditions, forgiving with watering; excellent for air purification.
Page: 24

Spider Plant

Low-maintenance, tolerates a range of conditions, produces, ideal for beginners, loves indirect light.
Page: 37

Snake Plant

Almost indestructible, prefers low light, minimal watering, excellent air purifier, and neglect tolerance.
Page: 38

RootGrowings The Houseplants Book   129

Madagascar Dragon Tree

Striking, slender leaves, prefers indirect light, moderate watering; great for adding a dramatic touch.
Page: 111

Lucky Bamboo

Symbol of good fortune, grows in water or soil, requires little care; perfect as a decorative piece.
Page: 26

Aloe vera

Low-maintenance, needs bright light, infrequent watering; great for treating burns and adding greenery.
Page: 48

6
HOUSEPLANTS FOR BEDROOM

Houseplants can turn any bedroom into a peaceful, natural retreat, easily growing in sunlight and lamplight. They add a lovely touch and help clean the air, making the room feel fresher and cozier, which is excellent for a good night's sleep. Perfect for all kinds of bedrooms!

Peace Lily

It purifies air, thrives in low light, and adds tranquility with white blooms, making it perfect for bedrooms.
Page: 29

Parlor Palm

Low-light lovers create a calming atmosphere, ideal for bringing a touch of nature to bedrooms.
Page: 28

English Ivy

It is an air purifier, prefers moderate light, and is excellent for hanging baskets in cozy bedroom settings.
Page: 22

Spider Plant

Easy care, purifies air, thrives in indirect light; suitable for adding greenery to bedrooms.
Page: 37

Wax Plant

Low-maintenance, thrives in bright, indirect light; perfect for bedrooms with its waxy, fragrant blooms.
Page: 41

Corn Plant

Low maintenance, air-purifying, prefers low to moderate light; adds a lush feel to bedrooms.
Page: 20

6
HOUSEPLANTS FOR BATHROOM

Houseplants in bathrooms add greenery and improve air quality, thriving in warm, humid environments with minimal care. Selections should be based on light, humidity, and temperature conditions. Low-light plants suit windowless areas, while ferns and air plants flourish near windows.

Asparagus Fern

Thrives in humidity and indirect light, perfect for warm, steamy bathrooms with its lush, feathery foliage
Page: 10

Croton

Loves bathroom humidity and needs bright, indirect light; its colored leaves enhance any bathroom's aesthetic.
Page: 53

Air Plant

It is ideal for humid bathrooms, requires no soil, and can hang anywhere, absorbing moisture and light effortlessly.
Page: 86

Snake Plant

Low light and humidity-friendly, air-purifying qualities make it an excellent choice for bathroom greenery.
Page: 38

Peace Lily

Flourishes in humid, low-light bathrooms, offering elegant white blooms and air-purifying capabilities.
Page: 29

Moth Orchid

Suited for the warm, humid bathroom conditions, they require indirect light for their elegant blooms.
Page: 67

6
HOUSEPLANTS FOR KITCHEN

Houseplants in kitchen decor enhance the ambiance and bring practical benefits. They purify the air and inject vibrant colors; some varieties yield fresh produce throughout the year. The right plant choice depends on each kitchen's specific light, humidity, and temperature conditions.

Golden Pothos

Ideal for kitchens, this hardy excels in various lighting, requires minimal care, and purifies air.
Page: 24

Heartleaf Philodendron

Perfect for kitchens, it thrives in indirect light, requires little attention, and brings vibrant greenery.
Page: 25

Spider Plant

Great for kitchens, adaptable to various light conditions, and requires minimal upkeep, adding charm.
Page: 37

Rubber plant

Striking in sunny kitchens requires minimal care, prefers bright light, and adds a bold, green statement.
Page: 35

ZZ Plant

Low-light and drought-tolerant, perfect for busy kitchens, with little maintenance needed.
Page: 43

African Violet

Brightens kitchens with colorful blooms; prefers indirect light and moderate watering, adding a pop of color.
Page: 46

6
HOUSEPLANTS FOR BALCONY

Plants and flowers transform apartment balconies with color and charm, creating an outdoor space as cozy as indoors. Regardless of size or sun exposure, whether spacious or compact, sunny or shaded, north or east-facing, the right mix of planters and plants enhances the balcony's appeal.

Hibiscus

Bright flowers perfect for sunny balconies; loves direct sunlight, regular watering, and adds tropical flair.
Page: 104

Aloe vera

Thrives in balcony sun, needs minimal watering; great for outdoor healing properties and sculptural beauty.
Page: 48

Ponytail palm

Unique, drought-tolerant, loves bright light; ideal for adding whimsy to sunny balconies with minimal care.
Page: 74

RootGrowings The Houseplants Book 137

Croton

Colorful leaves brighten balconies; prefers sunlight and moderate watering, perfect for a vibrant display.
Page: 53

Jade Plant

Hardy succulent for sunny balconies, requires little water; adds a touch of green elegance with minimal effort.
Page: 61

Areca palm

Lush, air-purifying, loves bright, indirect light; adds a tropical feel to balconies with regular watering.
Page: 50

6
HOUSEPLANTS FOR GOOD LUCK

Plants are valued for their aesthetic and health benefits, promoting calmness and well-being. In addition to these qualities, certain plants are also regarded as good luck symbols, particularly in Chinese culture, where they are famous for bringing fortune and prosperity.

Money Tree

Financial prosperity and good luck are associated with them. Perfect for offices or homes to enhance prosperity.
Page: 66

Lucky Bamboo

Symbolizes luck and prosperity; easy to grow in water or soil, ideal for adding positive energy to any space.
Page: 26

Jade Plant

Known as the 'money plant,' it's considered auspicious for wealth, making it a popular choice for home and office.
Page: 61

Chinese money plant

Round leaves symbolize abundance, are a popular gift for luck and prosperity, and are easy to care for indoors.
Page: 18

Ti Plant

Revered in many cultures for attracting good luck. Its vibrant leaves add a tropical flair and positive vibes.
Page: 78

Rubber Plant

Associated with abundance and happiness. Its large, glossy leaves purify the air and add elegance.
Page: 35

6
FRAGRANT HOUSEPLANTS

Plants are renowned for their air-purifying abilities, contributing to their popularity. Additionally, the charm of fragrant indoor houseplants lies in their ability to fill homes with delightful scents. Six sweet-smelling plants stand out for their ability with their pleasant aromas.

Cape jasmine

Offers lush, white blooms with a rich, sweet fragrance, perfect for infusing indoor spaces with a pleasant aroma.
Page: 91

Star Jasmine

It is known for its intensely fragrant, star-shaped flowers and is ideal for bringing a sweet, captivating scent indoors.
Page: 77

Lemon Balm

It emits a refreshing, lemony fragrance, great for kitchens or living areas, and is also known for its soothing properties.
Page: 108

RootGrowings The Houseplants Book 141

Madagascar Jasmine

Produces beautiful, fragrant white flowers, perfect for adding an exotic, sweet scent to any room.
Page: 112

Lily of the Valley

Delicate, bell-shaped flowers with a powerful, sweet fragrance, ideal for small spaces needing a scent boost.
Page: 64

Rosemary

Not only culinary, but its aromatic leaves also bring a fresh, herbaceous scent, great for kitchens or windowsills.
Page: 116

6 HOUSEPLANTS FOR OFFICE DESK

Plants can transform workspaces into serene, engaging areas. However, without proper care, desk plants may not thrive. A thoughtfully curated list of the best plants, specifically ideal for desk environments, is available, catering to seasoned gardeners and those new to plant care.

Chinese Money Plant

Perfect for desks, it thrives in indirect light and is easy to care for, and its leaves symbolize good fortune.
Page: 18

English Ivy

Ideal for desks, it purifies air and prefers indirect light; its trailing vines add a touch of elegance.
Page: 22

ZZ Plant

Low-light tolerant, minimal watering needed; sleek and sturdy, perfect for adding green to any office desk.
Page: 43

RootGrowings The Houseplants Book 143

Cooper's haworthia

Compact, perfect for office desks; it requires little light and water and adds a unique, textured aesthetic.
Page: 93

Prayer Plant

Eye-catching with its changing leaf positions, it thrives in indirect light and adds vibrant color to any desk.
Page: 30

Baby Rubber Plant

Perfect for desks with moderate light; low maintenance, offers lush, glossy leaves and a compact growth habit.
Page: 11

6
HOUSEPLANTS FOR DARK CORNERS

Indoor gardening can pose challenges with varied lighting conditions, yet a diverse array of plants specifically flourish in low-light environments. This ensures ample options for creatively greening spaces, even in settings lacking abundant, sunny windowsills.

Snake Plant

It is perfect for dark corners, requires minimal light, is virtually indestructible, and improves air quality.
Page: 38

Golden Pothos

Excellent for low light areas, easy to care for, with cascading vines that add a lush green touch to dim corners.
Page: 24

Arrow-Head Plant

Its lush greenery and vibrant growth make it adaptable to low light, making it perfect for adding life to darker corners.
Page: 9

Dieffenbachia

Its large, patterned leaves are ideal for low light, bringing a striking, lively presence to shadowy indoor spaces.
Page: 21

Cast Iron Plant

Extremely hardy, thrives in low light, perfect for the darkest corners, requiring minimal attention and care.
Page: 16

ZZ Plant

Perfect for dark areas, it requires minimal light and water and brings sleek, glossy leaves to any shadowy spot.
Page: 43

6
HOUSEPLANTS TO PLANT IN WATER

Many houseplants can thrive in water containers without soil. Just immerse the plant roots in water, ensuring the foliage stays above, and observe their growth. While not all houseplants are suitable for hydroponic conditions, several stunning options flourish in this unique setup.

Arrow-Head Plant

It thrives in water, perfect for hydroponic setups; lush foliage is ideal for adding greenery without soil.
Page: 9

Golden Pothos

They are excellently adapted to water, creating a stunning, leafy, water-based display with minimal fuss.
Page: 24

Wax Begonia

It is adaptable to water planting and offers vibrant flowers and foliage, perfect for brightening water gardens.
Page: 82

RootGrowings The Houseplants Book   147

Lucky Bamboo

Iconic for water growth and easy to maintain, it adds a peaceful, zen-like ambiance to any water setting.
Page: 26

Heartleaf Philodendron

It thrives in water, is easy to propagate, and has heart-shaped leaves, ideal for a water-based indoor garden.
Page: 25

Inch Plant

Perfect for water settings, fast-growing with striking purple foliage, ideal for vibrant water gardens.
Page: 60

SAFE FOR PETS HOUSEPLANTS

Welcome to our carefully selected garden of pet-safe houseplants! We understand that the joy of nurturing plants and the love for your furry companions go hand-in-hand.

The plants you'll find here have been chosen for their friendliness to pets. While we've done our best to ensure this list includes a wide variety of non-toxic options, it's important to remember that individual pets may react differently to certain plants. The appearance of plants can also vary, so always check the scientific name to confirm you're getting the exact type that's safe.

Low to Medium light plants

Aluminum Plant *Pilea cadierei*	Page-8	Parlor Palm *Chamaedorea elegans*	Page-28
Baby Rubber Plant *Peperomia obtusifolia*	Page-11	Prayer Plant *Maranta leuconeura*	Page-30
Baby's Tears *Soleirolia soleirolii*	Page-12	Polka dot plant *Hypoestes phyllostachya*	Page-32
Bird's Nest Fern *Asplenium Nidus*	Page-13	Rabbit's Foot Fern *Davallia*	Page-33
Boston Fern *Nephrolepis exaltata*	Page-14	Rattlesnake Plant *Calathea lancifolia*	Page-34
Cast Iron Plant *Aspidistra elatior*	Page-16	Spider Plant *Chlorophytum comosum*	Page-37
Chinese Money Plant *Pilea peperomioides*	Page-18	Watermelon peperomia *Peperomia argyreia*	Page-40
Christmas Cactus *Schlumbergera bridgesii*	Page-19	Wax Plant *Hoya carnosa*	Page-41
Nerve Plant *Fittonia albivenis*	Page-27		

Medium light plants

African Violet *Saintpaulia ionantha*	Page-46	Lipstick Plant *Aeschynanthus radicans*	Page-63
Areca Palm *Dypsis lutescens*	Page-50	Money Tree *Pachira aquatica*	Page-66
Cape Primrose *Streptocarpus spp.*	Page-51	Moth Orchid *Phalaenopsis*	Page-67
Common Staghorn Fern *Platycerium bifurcatum*	Page-52	Octopus plant *Tillandsia Caput Medusae*	Page-71
Flame Violet *Episcia cupreata*	Page-54	Ponytail Palm *Beaucarnea recurvata*	Page-74
Friendship Plant *Pilea involucrata*	Page-56	Scarlet Star *Guzmania lingulata*	Page-76
Gloxinia *Sinningia speciosa*	Page-57	Star Jasmine *Trachelospermum jasminoides*	Page-77
GoldFish Plant *Nematanthus gregarius*	Page-58	Urn plant *Aechmea fasciata*	Page-81

Medium to High light plants

Air Plant *Tillandsia*	Page-86	Lemon Balm *Melissa officinalis*	Page-108
Basil *Ocimum basilicum*	Page-88	Living Stones *Lithops*	Page-110
Cooper's haworthia *Haworthia cooperi*	Page-93	Madagascar Jasmine *Stephanotis floribunda*	Page-112
Common sage *Salvia officinalis*	Page-94	Majesty Palm *Ravenea rivularis*	Page-113
Dill *Anethum graveolens*	Page-97	Mexican snow ball *Echeveria elegans*	Page-114
Ghost Plant *Graptopetalum paraguayense*	Page-101	Rosemary *Salvia rosmarinus*	Page-116
Garden Marigold *Calendula officinalis*	Page-102	Thyme *Thymus vulgaris*	Page-122
Hibiscus *Hibiscus rosa-sinensis*	Page-104	Venus Flytrap *Dionaea muscipula*	Page-124
Hindu Rope *Hoya compacta*	Page-105	Zebra Haworthia *Haworthia fasciata*	Page-125
Kentia Palm *Howea forsteriana*	Page-107		

THE LAST LEAF

Let's Stay Connected
Thank you for joining us on this green journey through "RootGrowings The Houseplants Book." We hope it has inspired you to fill your life with more lush, leafy friends.

Follow Our Growth
For daily doses of foliage and tips on plant care, follow us on:
Instagram: @RootGrowings
TikTok: @RootGrowings
Facebook: RootGrowings Community

Share Your Plant Stories
We'd love to see your indoor jungles! Share your pictures and stories using #RootGrowings and join the global community of plant enthusiasts.

Feedback and Inquiries
Your thoughts are important to us. For feedback, questions, or just to say hello, reach out to us at:
Email: connect@rootgrowings.com
Website: www.rootgrowings.com

Workshops and Events
Keep an eye on our website and social media for announcements on upcoming workshops, webinars, and plant swap events in your area.

Join the Conversation
Do you have plant care tips or unique stories to share? Our blog and community forums are wonderful places to contribute your insights and learn from fellow plant lovers.
Together, let's make every home a greener, more serene space.

Printed in Great Britain
by Amazon